Praise for *True*

'The pleasure of this book is the way Lucinda Holdforth
gracefully and intelligently negotiates this well-worn
terrain and makes it her own . . . The story of a quiet
revolution written with a light, sure touch.'

The Age

'[A] quite remarkable piece of travel writing . . .
Passionate and compelling.'

Sydney Morning Herald

'Delightfully captivating . . . A truly lovely,
thoughtful and erudite journey.'

Sunday Telegraph

'There is no more perfect book for travellers to Paris than
Lucinda Holdforth's wonderfully erudite *True Pleasures*.'

Vogue Entertaining & Travel

'If you too dream of being Nancy Mitford, or perhaps
Madame de Pompadour or Colette, all of them living
in Paris as snug as oysters, this is the book for you.'

Canberra Times

'[A] fascinating study of an enduring city.'

Courier-Mail

'*True Pleasures* is more than biography or
memoir. It can be read as a gentle instruction manual
on how to look at life from a different view than
the usual run-of-the-mill perspectives.'

Limelight Magazine

LUCINDA HOLDFORTH

a memoir of

WOMEN IN PARIS

true pleasures

GREYSTONE BOOKS

Douglas & McIntyre Publishing Group

Vancouver/Toronto/Berkeley

Greystone Books
A division of Douglas & McIntyre Ltd.
2323 Quebec Street, Suite 201
Vancouver, British Columbia, Canada V5T 4S7
www.greystonebooks.com

Library and Archives Canada Cataloguing in Publication
Holdforth, Lucinda, 1963–
True pleasures : a memoir of women in Paris / Lucinda Holdforth.
Includes bibliographical references.

ISBN-13: 978-1-55365-129-1 (cloth)   ISBN-10: 1-55365-129-4 (cloth)
ISBN-13:978-1-55365-284-7 (paper)   ISBN-10: 1-55365-284-3 (paper)

1. Women—France—Paris—Biography. 2. Paris (France)—Biography. I. Title.
DC705.A1H64 2005   920.72′0944′36   C2005-900937-3

Published in Australia by Random House Australia Pty Ltd

Cover photograph © JK / Magnum Photos
Cover design by Stacey Noyes
Printed and bound in Canada by Friesens
Printed on acid-free paper that is forest-friendly (100% post-consumer recycled paper)
and has been processed chlorine free.
Distributed in the U.S. by Publishers Group West

Permission to quote from the following sources is gratefully acknowledged:
Richard Rand, *Intimate Encounters: Love and Domesticity in Eighteenth Century France* © 1977 by the
Trustee of Hood Museum of Art / Dartmouth College, reprinted with permission of Princeton
University Press. Extract from *My Apprenticeships* by Colette and translated by Helen Beauclerk
published by Secker & Warburg used by permission of The Random House Group Limited.
Extract from *Madame du Deffand and Her World* by Benedetta Craveri, translated from the Italian
by Teresa Waugh, reprinted by permission of David R. Godine, Publisher, Inc. (Copyright © 1982
by Benedetta Craveri, translated from the Italian by Teresa Waugh.) The Ballad of Lucy Jordan.
S. Silverstein © Evil Eye Music / Essex Music Australia, reprinted with permission. *The Letters of
Nancy Mitford and Evelyn Waugh* edited by Charlotte Mosley and *The Letters of Nancy Mitford* edited
by Charlotte Mosley reproduced by permission of Hodder and Stoughton Limited. Extract from
Voltaire's *Selected Writings,* edited by Christopher Thacker, reprinted by permission of The Everyman's
Library. Extract from *The Pursuit of Love* and *The Nancy Mitford Omnibus* reprinted by permission
of PDF on behalf of The Estate of Nancy Mitford © 1978, 1974, The Estate of Nancy Mitford.
Extract from *Selected Writings of Germaine de Staël* translated by Vivian Folkenflik reprinted by
permission of Columbia University Press.

Every effort has been made to trace accurate ownership of copyright text used in this book. Any
copyright owners who have inadvertently been omitted from acknowledgements and credits should
contact the publisher and omissions will be rectified in subsequent editions.

To Syd Hickman,
whose timing was perfect

Table of Contents

True pleasure for me can be found only in love,
in Paris or in power.

Germaine de Staël, 1803

1

Arrival

The mornin' sun touched lightly on the eyes of Lucy Jordan,
In a white suburban bedroom in a white suburban town,
As she lay there 'neath the covers dreaming of a thousand lovers,
Till the world turned to orange and the room went spinning round.
At the age of thirty-seven she realized she'd never ride through
Paris in a sports car with the warm wind in her hair.

'The Ballad of Lucy Jordan', Marianne Faithfull

ON A SPRING morning in 1944, Nancy Mitford was lying in bed feeling sorry for herself. At the age of forty, she disliked her life. Her marriage was a failure. She had written three minor novels, but their poor sales meant she was forced to work as an underpaid assistant in a London bookstore. She wanted to leave her job and write another novel, but couldn't quite afford to. War-time food rationing had left her dangerously thin, and now she was laid up with a severe bout of laryngitis.

On that day in London – bored, bed-ridden, frustrated – Nancy Mitford wrote her mother a letter. *I need a holiday*, she wrote. *I am so underpaid.* Then, out of the blue, she declared: *I am angling like mad for a job in Paris.* She emphasized that such a plan was all very nebulous – but you can tell that this is just a daughter's strategy to hose down a mother's mounting alarm.

It's the one-liner that really gives the game away. There it is, the next sentence all alone on the page, a single row of words like a song lyric: *Oh to live in Paris! I'd give anything.* And so Nancy Mitford gave voice to the ambition that would change her life.

Today, at dawn on a spring morning more than a half-century later, I stumble, drained and pale, through the plastic tubes of Charles de Gaulle airport. I've just stepped off a 24-hour flight. My skin is paper, my hair is wire, my travel-wear limp and stale.

A regal Algerian in his early thirties is my taxi driver. We talk a little; I try to energize my lazy Australian mouth to perform the acrobatics of French vowels and diphthongs. 'Australia?' he remarks. 'That's a long way away.' And, 'You love Paris, uh? Everyone loves Paris, of course.' Then, 'Me, no, I don't live here, it's too expensive – I commute here every day. It's OK.'

All of a sudden he says, shyly, tenderly, 'My wife has just had our first baby. A girl.' He holds up a small Polaroid – I lean forward to admire a coffee-colored baby with wisps of dark hair.

'She's beautiful,' I say. 'What is her name?'

'Scheherazade.'

I roll back in delight. 'The storyteller?' Of course. 'The *raconteuse*. How do you say her name again?'

He repeats the word with melting slowness, as if honey is rolling in his mouth: 'Sché-hé-ra-zade.'

It sounds so wonderful, so feminine and exotic, I repeat

it after him and I see him smiling at me proudly in his rearview mirror.

'Perhaps she will grow up to tell wonderful stories about her own life.'

'Yes,' he says. 'My wife believes so.'

Our conversation lapses as we draw closer to the city center. I wind down the dewy window as Paris resolves itself before my glad eyes: the sweep of the Seine, the creamy buildings, the domes and spires of the great monuments. Is it my imagination, or can I already smell the bittersweet coffee and buttery croissants?

We pull into rue de Normandie in the ancient Marais district. My destination is actually a little shop, converted into a tiny house. My friend Rachel is away at a conference in Brussels, but she has forwarded me her spare key. I fiddle awkwardly with locks and suddenly, I'm in.

The scene is comfortingly familiar: here are Rachel's red glass tulips, her American novels, her collection of black and white photographs . . . I knew them in Canberra, saw them again in her apartment on rue Maître Albert when I visited several years ago, watched the accretion of beautiful things. Even when we first met, two junior officers in the Department of Foreign Affairs and Trade, even then, Rachel had flair.

That's new, I see, that fabulous white *chaise longue*.

Like me, Rachel did not stay with the Department. We left Canberra within a year of each other following the election defeat of 1996. From the office of the vanquished Deputy Prime Minister, I went to Sydney to work for a management consulting firm; she came to Paris to work for the OECD. Now she advises global companies on trade issues.

On the dining table is a message in Rachel's black round hand on heavy white paper: *Dear Lu, If you are reading this you've made it!* She gives me careful instructions on the lights, the heating, the TV, the nearest Metro station and the local food markets.

A narrow curved stairway leads up to the bedrooms. My bed is dressed in lemon-scented white linen, big fluffy pillows for reading, space in the cupboard for my clothes and books, even flowers and a quaint history of the Marais district on my bedside table.

It's getting warm. I take a shower, and the steam lifts the airplane's stale odors from my skin. Then I lie on the white bed as the muted Parisian light flickers through the window and the progressively more purposeful street noises rise up.

⚜

When I joined the management consulting firm, I sailed in on a tide of stockmarket excess. Business was booming and the partners were feeling benevolent. They were in the mood to talk about quality. They were ready to be excellent. So I was employed to help the management consultants communicate more effectively with their clients: together we would make a team of *compelling communicators*.

I was grateful for this task because it brought me home to Sydney and restarted my life. I made good money. Sometimes I had the opportunity to travel: I ran training courses in Japan and China. Unfortunately, however, I knew deep down that the job didn't matter a damn. I helped the consultants spin a good yarn for the clients, but I didn't believe a word of it. I just couldn't think of anything better to do.

After a couple of years, the atmosphere at work

changed. The tide of largesse was ebbing. Luxuries were being cut back, and I was, well, a luxury. As the human resources manager reminded me sourly, I was not a profit center, but a *cost* center.

One day, about a year ago, my boss called me into his office.

'I'd like you to think about taking on a change of role,' he said. 'Moving into the consulting stream.'

I nearly burst out laughing. 'Become a consultant? Me? But I can't count!' (It was bad enough working for the Deputy Prime Minister, who also happened to be Finance Minister; I couldn't even wield a pocket calculator with confidence.)

He dismissed this reservation with an imperial wave of the hand. 'Doesn't matter,' he said. 'You've got the brains. You'd be the boss, the strategist; the junior consultants would crunch the numbers.'

'You know,' he added, coaxingly, 'you would be on track to become a partner. You could make a lot of money. I mean, a lot,' he concluded. I could see he felt this argument was highly persuasive. He didn't know that as far as I was concerned, I was already making a lot of money.

'OK,' I said. 'Let me have a think about it.'

But thinking about it just made me feel tired. I recognized the signs. Another phase in my life was coming to an end, which simply meant I had to prepare myself for more change, more new beginnings. This was not a cause for exhilaration, but, at thirty-five, for weary deflation. More of the same old quest – if only I could put my finger on what the quest was all about.

One useful insight was revealed to me by that unsettling conversation with my boss. Even though I really liked the idea of a lot of money, money just wasn't enough. It seemed I was greedy: I wanted more than money.

Gradually, things began to stir inside me. I came to understand that this time it wasn't going to be enough for me to find a new job, or change cities again, or scale my ambitions up – or down – a notch, or even just mark time. All my life, it seemed, I'd been trying for something better than this, something *bigger* than this.

⚜

Most of us, I guess, when contemplating a life change, turn to the accepted sources of advice in the modern world: friends, family, mentors, colleagues, therapists, career advisers, self-help guides. And so, during this period of professional and personal stalemate, did I.

But it didn't seem to work; I felt I was crawling blindly within the same old parameters of discussion. There was only so far I could get with conversations about career choices; about men, marriage and babies; about Sydney property values; about work–life balance. At the back of my mind I couldn't help but suspect that this seemingly endless conversation was, itself, part of the problem. I felt a bit like that character in *The Truman Show*, wondering if, somewhere out there, real life started from a completely different set of premises.

So – and it seems inevitable in retrospect – that's when the reading started. Or perhaps I should say resumed, for at first I turned to some of my oldest friends, to Colette and Nancy Mitford and Edith Wharton. I re-read their novels and their memoirs, their biographies and their essays. The retreat to books had always consoled me, and these writers in particular had always had something to say to me about being a woman, about crafting a beautiful life.

Then, almost without pausing, I moved on to their life stories. And I rediscovered that these three had created their works of art within a few miles of each other, in the heart of Paris. Why hadn't I thought about this before?

The life stories of these Paris-based writers led in turn to the women of Paris whom *they* had admired: there was Madame de Pompadour, immortalized in biography by Nancy Mitford; George Sand, who fascinated Edith Wharton; and the notorious nineteenth-century courtesans, inspirations to Colette. And through these came others, a parade of *Parisiennes*. They began to fascinate me, these women, so much so that their past soon became a lot more interesting to me than my present.

On early morning plane trips to Melbourne, business travellers would prominently peruse the *Financial Review*: I was buried deep in *Mademoiselle Libertine: A Portrait of Ninon de Lanclos*. Friends looked surprised when I told them I hadn't yet read Martin Amis's prize-winner, but that I *could* warmly recommend *The Duchess Hortense: Cardinal Mazarin's Wanton Niece*. One day a senior colleague discovered me in a café with *The Passionate Exiles: A dual biography of Mme Récamier and Mme De Staël*. He could barely smother his alarm.

Through this strange period of reading and working and contemplating their past and my future, the women of Paris – wild, noble, brave, bad, strong, foolish – came to represent important things to me: the grand scale that an individual life can achieve; the beautiful arc that a finished life can describe; the radiant, limitless scope of female potentiality.

And I found that the individual stories of these women's lives did not exist in isolation, but connected across time and space, like threads in the grand narrative tapestry that is the story of Paris itself.

⚜

And so, at last, I find myself light and tired on the spare bed at Rachel's place. I quit the job, of course: my diary is empty. But my heart feels full. I roll onto my side, but I can't sleep. The tingle of adrenaline floods my veins. Like Scheherazade's wakeful emperor, I crave the stories.

❧ 2 ❧

Great Dames

O unfathomable, inexhaustible Paris . . .

Colette

THERE'S A REASON why people write songs about Paris in the spring. And it's not just because of the chestnut blossoms or the glossy new vegetables or the open-air cafés. It's because in springtime, Paris achieves the optimal balance between her two most essential attributes: elegance and enjoyment. In spring a woman can wear stylish clothes with a tilt at holiday freedom. She can stroll, as I do, with a jaunty air along the rue de Bretagne, in the bluish morning light, wearing a structured jacket with a little T-shirt beneath (in case the day turns balmy) and a sweater in her bag (in case it turns cool). Spring in Paris has a woman's strong and shifting moods.

Rue de Bretagne, at the unfashionable end of the Marais, will be my shopping street for the next three weeks. I acquaint myself with my preferred local *boulangerie* (one of three, but this one has the best *croissants beurre*, according to Rachel's note), the *fromagerie* for cheese, the local Nicolas wine shop, the fruit and vegetable vendors. I absorb the vivid colors, inhale the rich odors, but there's no rush to taste or try. This timeless Paris scene has been here forever; it will wait for me just a little longer.

Heading towards the river, the Marais district becomes both more enchanting and more imposing with every step. It has detail and scale. I have to keep crossing the road to gaze through small shop windows at a delicately embroidered handbag, or a witty lampshade, or a frail dress, or to gain a little distance and perspective on a grand seventeenth-century mansion. I am already trying to remember what I have read about each building – attempting to superimpose my fictional and historical idea of Paris onto the real thing. I pass one of Rachel's favorite shops on rue des Francs-Bourgeois – it sells rack after rack of old postcards telling their own black and white version of the history of Paris.

As I breathe the cool air, I feel my chest expand and my heart lift. I have always looked persistently forwards at life, peering anxiously into the void. Too often I've rushed headlong towards it. In this, I guess, I've been a creature of my times. Modern society is all about negating the past. We are encouraged to abandon whatever is old, or used, or private, or can no longer be measured in dollars. Instead we are enjoined to live in a state of nagging dissatisfaction, downgrading our personal belongings and experiences in order to seek out new and better ones in the marketplace. Even our own ageing bodies are subject to this relentless rejection of that which isn't fresh and new. Our eyes are raised to a golden future, purchased over and over again, and yet never, quite, achieved.

But now I feel myself easing back from this anxious modernity. It seems I am beginning to learn the solace and the lessons of history. These past few months of reading have lengthened and clarified my perspective. History takes life backwards – and allows us to see the future in a different way. Within its grand schemas individual lives seem less important, and yet somehow, or perhaps for that very reason, more beautiful. History humbles and ennobles us all at the same time.

On this morning in Paris, among the timeless shop-keepers and the eternal streets and the ancient buildings, I can thank the women of Paris for another insight. For many of them, like me, things didn't necessarily make sense from day to day. Life was a mysterious and elusive business. But they held their nerve, and time vindicated their courage.

It's springtime, and the season unfolds with orderly beauty. I relax.

⚜

What a great old dame she is. Weaving my way through the crowd outside Notre-Dame Cathedral, I pause and gaze upwards at the vast stone facade. She has been thoroughly cleaned in recent years and the facelift has worked wonders for her. Even the gargoyles look happier. I don't go inside the church – it's all a bit too gloomy and bats-in-the-belfry for my taste (I prefer the delicacy of Sainte-Chapelle) – but I wander behind her great bulk and cross over the bridge. Here's a very traditional café from where, in a window seat, I can look across to the back of Notre-Dame. From this angle I can see the old lady's flying buttresses, the boning and corsetry and stiffened petticoats which keep her aloft and intact.

This great dame resides in the historic and geographic heart of Paris, at the center of a city which, like a magnet, has attracted grand women from around the world. The roll-call in the past century alone includes Maria Callas, Nancy Mitford, Edith Wharton, Jane Birkin, Olivia de Havilland, Charlotte Rampling, Petula Clarke, Anaïs Nin, Lee Miller, Isadora Duncan, Mata Hari, Marlene Dietrich, Gertrude Stein, Josephine Baker, Janet Flanner, Djuna Barnes . . . each of these women migrated to Paris at some time during their lives, and many of them made their permanent homes here.

Why did they come to Paris? Love, of course, has always played its part. *She met a Frenchman, she fell in love, she moved to Paris.* (Many times, of course, she came to Paris to find love with a woman.) Nancy Mitford's love of Paris became a passion after she commenced her love affair with Frenchman Gaston Palewski. But there was always more to it than love alone, I think. Paris provided a space for women to free themselves, if they chose, from the tangled web of romantic and familial relationships. It was where they could be free to *be* themselves. Free even to *reinvent* themselves.

Gertrude Stein put it this way:

And so I am an American
and I have lived half my life in Paris,
not the half that made me but the half
in which I made what I made.

The chance to make whatever you choose of your life – that's the promise Paris offered to Gertrude Stein and other women. This was a city in which a woman might define herself, and be accepted by society at her own definition. It's a captivating idea – that you can transcend your past, your genealogy, your childhood experiences, or even the heavy weight of your own culture.

But it took me some years to understand the special and feminine allure of Paris.

The first time I came to this city I was a junior Australian diplomat on my way to a first posting in Belgrade. It was winter, and even though I marched briskly along the boulevards, my body seemed to be freezing upwards from my feet. Far from being the tenderly romantic city of fame, Paris was even colder than I felt. Those neutral walls seemed indifferent to the eager tourist. They weren't elaborately worked like New York skyscrapers, inviting you to tilt back your neck and admire. Nor were they low enough to encourage a little discreet peeking. I trudged for bland miles past those damned Parisian walls, designed, it seemed, for one purpose only – to keep the uninvited (me) out.

I was staying with colleagues in the Australian Embassy residence in the 15th *arrondissement*, a modernist building designed like a military bunker complete with slit windows. Not only did these low-slung windows eliminate all traces of sunshine from the apartment, they formed, a resident said sourly, perfect machine gun nests if ever we wanted to target the enemy buildings on the Right Bank.

Of course, I visited the famous tourist spots. Impressive though they were, they didn't appeal. New Year's Eve under the Eiffel Tower was metallically cold, made worse by loud youngsters popping firecrackers. The Louvre seemed far too big and too intimidating for me to absorb.

Even Mona Lisa's smile seemed more like an anxious smirk directed at the flashbulbs of Japanese tourists.

But there were compensating pleasures. There was a bistro on the Left Bank with its blackboard menu and white cloths and bustling Sunday lunch. There was Angelina's on rue de Rivoli with its faded murals and elegant, tiny old ladies. The hot chocolate was so soupy and the Mont Blanc so chestnutty-sweet it nearly made winter worthwhile. There was a visit to Australian friends living in a furnished apartment. I was struck by the dilapidated elegance of the creaking lift and the threadbare tapestry chairs and the big-nosed nineteenth-century ancestors staring disapprovingly at me from faded gilt frames. This worn-out grandeur was amusing, and appealing. Even so, I didn't feel that I had connected with Paris: I didn't, somehow, get it.

Which was curious in a way, because I had studied French at school and university. I should have felt more at home than I did. On the other hand, whatever I learned, it left me supremely unfit to appreciate Paris.

I remember a sun-filled classroom of schoolgirls led by Sister Jude, a tiny Catholic nun dressed in the old-style habit with long black veil and tiny black lace-up shoes peeping out from under her long robe. She was, intermittently, teaching us the French language, but more often became carried away by her enthusiasm for French culture. Or at least, one aspect of it. 'Just think, girls,' she would murmur, her smooth face shining, 'just think of the French and their love of God.' Inward groans all round.

'Wherever you go in France, even in the poorest villages, you will see a beautiful church. Because no matter how poor the peasants were, they cheerfully gave their money to the priests. They wanted to build the best house in the village for the Lord . . .' French peasants were thereafter regarded by all of Sister Jude's students as exceptionally silly.

A few years later I was a first-year student of French at Sydney University. Semiotics and deconstruction were the rage – we didn't read French history, we deconstructed narratives; we didn't savor French literature, we analyzed texts. It was Barthes not Baudelaire. Lacan not La Roche-foucauld. In fact, it was a nightmare. Studying French at Sydney University nearly put me off France for life.

I learned a lot of things from my education – I even learned passable French – but I didn't learn the first thing about the history and culture of Paris. I had no real basis for understanding this great, complex urban organism. When I first came to Paris, I was just another tourist, with slightly better French.

⚜

Some years passed before I returned. By now I was nearly thirty years old, and feeling bruised by life. I had a good job, working as an adviser and speechwriter to the Deputy Prime Minister, but I was not entirely at ease in the role. There was something depressing about politics a lot of the time. I had a nice boyfriend, but it was a difficult relation-ship, and often strained. In fact, I felt so raw and fragile I asked my friend and former colleague Ellen to meet me at the airport at 7 am – a huge request, in hindsight. There she was, a serene figure in the early morning hubbub, greeting me in her beautiful low voice, shepherding me through the crowd.

Because Ellen was an Australian diplomat, I was back staying in the Australian bunker and, though I was incred-ibly grateful for the privilege, it had to be admitted that it was as depressing as ever. Ellen, however, had filled her flat with dramatic modern art and Perrier Jouet champagne and red-corseted Yohji Yamamoto suits and pleated Issey Miyake shirts. Her stylishness didn't redeem the building, but it enlivened the dark, cavernous apartment.

And, anyway, this time I was in a different Paris, summer Paris, a completely new city. And this was Paris seen through Ellen's eyes, the eyes of someone who knew and loved the city. She took me on a journey through *her* Paris.

But first Ellen had to make me presentable by giving me a few lessons in French culture. As we walked into her local *boulangerie*, Ellen leaned in to me. 'Don't smile,' she murmured.

'Pardon?'

'You smile too much: they'll think you are an American.'

This threw me. 'And what's wrong with smiling?'

'The French think it's infantile to smile at complete strangers; it's like a baby looking for approval.'

I felt a touch resentful. I wanted to say: so are you saying I'm infantile? Are you? *Are you?* But instead I confined myself to, 'So, what, I should be cold and cool?'

'You should be extremely polite. When you enter a shop you should say, very clearly, as the French do, "Bonjour Madame" or "Monsieur" and "Merci, Madame, au revoir". when you leave. The French keep a dignified and extremely civil distance. It's French manners, and very good they are too.' Yes, a smug tone was definitely creeping into her voice. But I dutifully changed facial gears from smile to neutral.

A few hours later, I blurted: 'Hang on, you were smiling non-stop at that waiter!'

'Yes, I was, wasn't I.' Ellen arched her eyebrow and gently swished her wine glass.

'Isn't it funny, after a while, you don't need to follow the rules anymore, don't ask me why.' I smarted at Ellen's infuriating complacency, but the weird thing was, she was right. As soon as I stopped expecting French people to smile at me – they did. It was as if I had tuned into a perverse social rhythm.

After I got the hang of not-smiling/smiling, after I had learned to enter and exit boutiques and cafés with brief but elaborate courtesy, Paris became a much more friendly place.

In those few weeks Ellen took time off work and we walked for miles, criss-crossing bridges and detouring down lane-ways, poking around nineteenth-century arcades and emerging into great residential squares. We went to large famous shops and tiny specialist ones. We bought three pairs of Robert Clergerie shoes. We dined at a traditional brasserie where old ladies fed their dogs under the table, posed at a party with Japanese fashion designers and invaded a Cambodian noodle house for a late-night feast. We sipped *kirs* outside Deux Magots and watched the gay parade down Boulevard Saint-Germain. We ate lunch with Australian artists and dinner with French management consultants.

In Nancy Mitford's *The Pursuit of Love*, heroine Linda falls in love with Paris when she sees it with her lover, Fabrice.

'How fortunate you are to live in such a town,' she said to Fabrice. 'It would be impossible to be very unhappy here.'

'Not impossible. One's emotions are intensified in Paris – one can be more happy and also more unhappy here than in any other place. But it is always a positive source of joy to live here and there is nobody so miserable as a Parisian in exile from his town. The rest

of the world seems unbearably cold and bleak to us, hardly worth living in.'

I was beginning to get the idea.

At one party Ellen and I encountered two young artists and formed an instant bond. Their names were Felix and Kim. Felix, with his dark eyes and curls was, I assumed, from the south of France; Kim, from Korea, was his smiling slender girlfriend. One night Felix took us to Les Bains, an ultra-chic nightclub owned by his brother. A party was being held to celebrate Jean-Paul Gaultier's winter men's collection. We were having a wonderful time, drinking champagne, mingling, checking out the beautiful models. At some stage late in the night Ellen was being monopolized by an Italian hairdresser who resembled a decadent Caravaggio youth, and I found myself chatting with Felix through a tunnel of dance music. I heard him mention Tunisia. For reasons I can now only ascribe to an excess of champagne, I assumed he was referring to Ellen's recent unhappy holiday there.

I pulled a dramatic face. 'HELLHOLE!' I shouted at him, helpfully.

Felix looked a little surprised.

'NEVER GO THERE, NO GOOD,' I yelled. I clutched my stomach and writhed theatrically. 'GET SICK AS DOG.'

Felix leaned in close and put his lips to my ear. 'No,' he said. 'I AM Tunisian.'

Then he roared with laughter as an expression of utmost horror spread across my face. After that we became firm friends.

Felix and Kim turned up at Ellen's place the night before I was due to leave and demanded that I stay in Paris an extra day so that both Ellen and I could attend their wedding. At the town hall of the 16th *arrondissement*, the ceremony took exactly two minutes. Afterwards, to my considerable surprise, the mayor in his splendid robes passed around a bowl for donations (for what? I wondered). Outside, Felix and Kim posed for photos in their matching white pant suits as the hot day glowed around them.

The wedding party was held at the home of Felix's brother. Within the bland creamy walls of a Parisian mansion, the courtyard was strewn with blossoms and the inside of the courtyard doors were painted vivid blue. Every now and then the blue doors would swing open and white-coated delivery men would surge through with another bunch of flowers, or trays of oysters and smoked salmon or a teetering *croquembouche* – the wedding cake. For the first time I had been invited – on my own account, and not just as Ellen's friend – to participate in the life of Paris, to take my place on the stage and perform my bit part in the drama of the city. And it felt like theater: it was an occasion with the zest and unlikely joy of a Shakespearean comedy, with a multi-ethnic cast of photographers, fashion designers, tarot readers, makeup artists, ancient socialites and beautiful young things tangling themselves up in absorbing sub-plots over the course of a long summer night.

Finally, Paris began to make sense to me. A city that was formal and frivolous, ancient and ageless, intensely conservative and furiously modern. That night, with the joyful newlyweds and the floating air and the music and the silly conversations in four languages, I felt a tender connection with the city. I knew that I would keep coming back.

I left Ellen and Paris and returned to Canberra, to an election that the Labor Party inevitably lost. And then my boyfriend dumped me. But I had found a kernel of something special in myself again – a little bit of confidence, an ounce of hope.

For, no matter what happened, and as for so many before me, the cliché was a treasure and a promise: *I'd always have Paris . . .*

⚜

As I sit here with my notebook and a list of magical addresses, it now seems hard to believe that in all those previous visits to Paris it never once occurred to me to track down the haunts of my favorite women writers. Ellen once pointed out Colette's home in the Palais Royal, but I felt no particular surge of connection or recognition. I guess at that stage I had no idea what the interior of the building looked like: there was nothing in her remark for my imagination to take hold of. (Today, of course, I can vividly imagine the close, cozy room with its red walls and mirrors and colorful glass paperweights – and the purple-maned lioness lying on her divan.)

Paris is one of those cities you could unpeel for a lifetime and still not succeed in uncovering all its variety, its multiple personalities. There's seventeenth-century Paris, revolutionary Paris, Bonaparte's Paris, existentialist Paris, *avant-garde* Paris. The real Paris, modern Paris, with its *clochards* and dog poo and ethnic vibe and snobbery and local corruption, lives in complex partnership with the Paris of yesterday, the Paris of many yesterdays. And the Paris of many imaginations, for Paris is an idea as much as a place.

In the early nineteenth century, when George Sand arrived in Paris from the provinces, she moved several times until she found just the location she had in mind. For she, too, was searching to realize a personal idea of Paris.

I . . . was soon settled on Quai Saint-Michel in one of the garrets of the big house on the corner of the block, at the end of the bridge, opposite the Morgue. There I had three small, very clean rooms leading to a balcony from which I had an extensive view of the Seine, and where I could contemplate, face to face, the gigantic monuments of Notre-Dame, Saint-Jacques-la-Boucherie, Sainte-Chapelle, and others. I had sky, water, air, swallows, rooftop greenery; I did not feel too much part of modern Paris, which would not have suited my taste nor my resources, but more so in the picturesque and poetic Paris of Victor Hugo, the Paris of the past.

George Sand sought the Paris that corresponded to her emotional state and her artistic aspirations. In her little Gothic attic she found the perfect place to invent herself as a Romantic heroine and to explore Paris, liberty and love. And Paris made space for George Sand, adjusting to accommodate her. It eddied and swirled, widened its flow. It gave her room to change.

The Paris of my imagination is a site of pleasure and history and beauty. It's a place to recharge myself as a woman. Each time I come back here it's like greeting an older woman friend, one who is rather grand and imperious – a great dame, in fact – who likes me to look my best, to have my wittiest conversation to hand and to be on my toes all the time.

I finish my morning coffee and gaze back across to Notre-Dame, the greatest dame of all. But her fixity, her grand monolithic bulk, doesn't enchant me. It's the flesh and blood women who fascinate: women in flux, in progress, in self-discovery, in the act of creation.

～ 3 ～

Place des Vosges

As life is an art in France, so woman is an artist.

Edith Wharton

EVEN IN PARIS, one of the world's most beautiful cities, Place des Vosges in the 4th *arrondissement* is *so* beautiful I want to laugh out loud. I step off teeming rue Saint-Antoine into l'Hôtel de Sully, linger at the overflowing bookshop, dogleg through the courtyard, and, *voilà!* here I am. It's late on a spring morning a few days after my arrival, and the Place presents itself to me like a gift.

It's not that Place des Vosges is either grand or intimidating. In fact, with its rose and cream bricks, its shady arcades, its quadrangled garden, Place des Vosges is built on a decidedly human scale. I come from Sydney, a new place, where old buildings are routinely condemned as dysfunctional. Yet this piece of urban design, at nearly four hundred years old, works beautifully. Thirty-six houses stand tall, slim and solid around the square. The galleries and arcades below provide shelter for strolling and space for art galleries and boutiques. There's a Michelin three-star restaurant at one end of the Place and a luxury hotel at the other. On the garden benches are the usual lovers, the mothers gently rocking their prams, the old men with their newspapers. A clutch of tourists look around with pleased expressions, as if the square had been designed exactly to their careful specifications. It's that kind of place.

I thread my way across to a corner café, Ma Bourgogne, where I order a glass of soft red wine, and settle down to watch and to daydream. I am gazing at the present, but I am thinking about the past. Here, I think, *here* is where it all began.

When foreigners want to understand the French, they generally head to Versailles. That's because at Versailles, it is said, Louis XIV, the Sun King himself, invented French culture. He commenced renovations on a family hunting lodge in 1661, and he progressively moved the court there from Paris from about 1674. Louis XIV made Versailles a gilded cage for his captive aristocrats. He kept the ruling class entirely occupied with pleasure and ceremony: he made his courtiers so busy that they had neither time nor inclination to plot against him. The Sun King established an elaborate social code, which, through war and conquest, he exported to the rest of Europe. But Louis XIV didn't invent French culture; he just borrowed it.

Over here on my left is number 20 Place des Vosges. This is where a bride arrived from Italy to stay in the house of her father-in-law, sometime around 1590. Her name was Catherine de Vivonne, the new Marquise de Rambouillet. From courtly Italy with its chivalrous traditions she had landed in rough-hewn France. Place des Vosges, then known as Place Royale, was still under construction. Its primary use was as a rowdy military parade ground. Residents awoke at dawn to the metal clashes of duellists fighting for sport or honor. Life in Paris was altogether medieval and martial. *Worst of all*, thought the young bride, *the houses!* Grand homes were designed like feudal hunting lodges, with drafty baronial spaces and blood-red walls.

So la Marquise commissioned a house, a perfect house. Her blue, white and gold reception room was intimate, scaled down, with little alcoves to encourage private exchanges. La Marquise, in her lilting Italian accent, called the reception space her *salone,* and it became, of course, the first salon. The guest list was pruned to privilege talent, beauty, honor and wit: only the greatest artists and writers were invited; the bravest soldiers; the most beautiful, pious women. Wives and husbands were not automatically included – no free riders, thanks – and this no doubt contributed a flirtatious element to the conversation. For the first time, women became socially central. Their role was to guide, to instruct, to inspire, to elevate – the most refined were known as *les précieuses.* Men aspired to become *honnêtes hommes* – honorable, cultivated, natural and, most important of all, socially graceful. At the core of this little society was a new idea – the art of living itself, *savoir vivre.*

Under one roof, La Marquise de Rambouillet brought together all the elements that we associate with Paris today: the elevation to art of food, conversation, clothes and love. The historian Vincent Cronin said of Place Royale: *This square can be said to mark the change from the rough masculine society of Henri IV to the witty society revolving around certain gifted or beautiful women which still prevails today.*

Just over on the other side of the square at number 1 is the birthplace of la Marquise de Rambouillet's most famous guest, Madame de Sévigné. Madame de Sévigné sparkled. She was funny, spirited and worldly. Later she lived around the corner in what is now Musée Carnavalet, appropriately the museum of Paris history. Her letters embody the French idea of *esprit* – wit, intellect and spirit combined.

Time for another wine, and now I look directly across the square to where it exits to rue du Pas-de-la-Mule. Just around the corner lived the most influential courtesan of the seventeenth century. She used to ride into this square on a little sedan-chair carried by her menservants. Her name was Ninon de Lanclos.

Ninon de Lanclos wasn't like the *précieuses*: she wasn't elevated or precious. She was an epicurean – a philosopher of judicious pleasure. *All good sense should lead in the direction of happiness*, she believed. Unlike the pious women of la Marquise de Rambouillet's salon, Ninon demanded all the liberties and responsibilities available to men. Her motto was: *Make me a gentle man* [honnête homme]*, but never a chaste woman . . .*

One of Ninon's early admirers was Cardinal Richelieu. He lived here in Place Royale too, at number 21 – just behind me in fact, and, see, there's a plaque on the shop-front. He offered Ninon a fortune to become his mistress. She declined: the outrageous sum of money was too much from a lover but not enough from a man she didn't love.

As she matured, Ninon became so respectable that society ladies would send their sons to study at her school of gallantry. We can thank Ninon for the Frenchman's romantic reputation: she turned gauche young men into ardent and skilful lovers. *It takes a hundred times more skill to make love than to command an army*, she used to say.

But the wittiest men in Paris gathered in Ninon's salon for the conversation alone. Playwright Molière was her close friend, maxim writer La Rochefoucauld a regular and she was the first to recognize the genius in the boy Voltaire, leaving him a bequest in her will. Each of these men, whose fame in the English-speaking world eclipsed hers, hurried through this lovely square to visit Ninon de Lanclos in her home around the corner.

Centuries later Simone de Beauvoir wrote:

The Frenchwoman whose independence seems . . . the most like that of a man is perhaps Ninon de Lanclos, seventeenth-century woman of wit and beauty. Paradoxically, those women who exploit their femininity to the limit create for themselves a situation almost equivalent to that of a man . . . Free in behaviour and conversation, they can attain – like Ninon de Lanclos – to the rarest intellectual liberty.

So it was here, in and around Place des Vosges, that a group of women took charge, creating a society which valued beauty, love, sex, art and culture. What strikes me now, as I sit here in this perfect, unchanged space with the strolling couples and the playing children and elegant shops, is how intensely *urban* it is. And it's curious, because I've noticed lately how often the idea of the 'art of living' is associated with retreat from the city, with a pastoral fantasy: a villa in Tuscany perhaps, or a charming shack on an unspoiled beach. But in the seventeenth century, *l'art de vivre* was an urban idea, and the women who embraced it weren't the least bit interested in retreating from the world; far from it. They were re-shaping the social order, placing themselves at the center of civilized life.

When I first began reading about the salonnières I couldn't suppress some disbelief. Come on, surely not, could these women really have enjoyed so much freedom? But they did. Many of them lived as single, independent people with a rich circle of friends, social activities and civic engagement. One salon hostess was Mademoiselle de Scudéry, who wrote popular romantic novels. She never married; indeed, she never aspired to: *I should have been deeply chagrined had I ever been faced with a union*, she said bluntly. Madame de Sévigné was wealthy, beautiful and widowed at twenty-five. She point-blank refused ever to marry again. Another resolute spinster was the cousin of Louis XIV, La Grande Mademoiselle. Louis XIV exiled his stubborn cousin several times from Paris because she refused to marry the candidates he selected for her; she too died a single woman.

And there was Ninon herself, Mademoiselle Libertine, who had a son but never married. She only slept with one of her five rich *payeurs* if and when she felt like it. Even into old age she had a stable of *martyrs* from which Ninon would occasionally select a robust and handsome *favori* – her affairs usually lasted no more than three months. As Ninon said: *A sensible woman must never take a husband without the consent of her reason, nor lovers without the advice of her heart*. It seems Ninon, in common with a number of women of her era, never quite found a good enough reason to marry. In our modern society, life as an older single woman carries some social disadvantage. But in those days in Paris, for women of a certain class, it was the route to moral, intellectual and social liberty.

Louis XIV grew up in Paris in this world of witty, diverse and sure-footed women. And when he established Versailles as his seat of power, he crystallized the feminine values nurtured in Paris salons into a system of etiquette, establishing the foundations of modern social discourse. Later, Versailles ossified into sterile ceremony under the King's long reign, but in Paris the salons continued to sparkle and evolve under the guidance of a few exceptional women.

Now, warmed by the wine and the sunshine, I stroll around Place des Vosges. I can feel the spirit of the past all around me. There's number 1, where the high-spirited Madame de Sévigné was born; and number 6, where another courtesan, Marion Delorme, introduced Ninon to society; and there's number 21 where Cardinal Richelieu lived. I can feel the heavy silks of cardinals and courtesans. I can hear the quiet laughter and *bons mots* and the whispered plans for assignations. The murmurs in my head mingle with the laughter from a young couple on a park bench.

And I remember something else about the salonnières. They were fascinated by human nature. They liked nothing more than to analyze and describe the complex workings of the human heart. In each other's salons they polished their ideas until they shone. Open a book of aphorisms and you will find it full of *maximes*, epigrams and *bons mots* by Madame de Sévigné and her cousin, Bussy-Rabutin; La Rochefoucauld and his mistress Madame de Lafayette; Mademoiselle de Scudéry and La Bruyère.

A jealous man always finds more than he is looking for, murmurs Mademoiselle de Scudéry. *When a plain-looking woman is loved it can only be very passionately; for either her influence over her lover is irresistible, or she has secret charms more powerful than those of beauty*, whispers La Bruyère. *If love is judged by its physical effects it looks more like hatred than friendship*, sneers La Rochefoucauld, who took a dark view of human nature. It gives me a shiver of ghostly pleasure to hear these wise, worldly, tart voices relay their thoughts direct to me from the seventeenth-century salons. It's an injection of moral sophistication, a relieving antidote to modern simplifications.

I like to imagine I could hold my own in a conversation with these sharp talkers, but I suspect I would come out badly. Modern life makes you sloppy and self-indulgent. We tend to think that self-revelation constitutes good conversation. But even though I might find the demands of this group alarming, I would welcome the tonic. I'd try to be swift and subtle. I'd try to be lucid and unflinching. I wouldn't succeed, but it would take me up a few notches.

Up the road from here, in rue de Beauce, which was then – and still remains – one of the less fashionable parts of the Marais district, lived Mademoiselle de Scudéry. She created a strange, marvelous work of art. It is a map, with a broad river running horizontally across the top, a stream splitting the map vertically, and, dotted here and there, lakes and villages. But this is no battlefield plan – or perhaps it is, for it represents a survey, an inquiry into the very nature of love. The supreme destination at the bottom of the map is the Kingdom of Tenderness, and the direct path to this goal tracks the downward flowing stream, traversing peaceful villages like *Grand Coeur*, *Sincérité*, *Billet-doux* and *Tendresse*. But there are by-ways and pitfalls too, traps for the foolish or faithless traveller, like *Perfidie*, *Complaisance*, and the *Lac d'Indifférence*.

When I first saw a picture of *La Carte de Tendre* I thought: how astonishing, with its bivalved structure, it looks rather like a map of the heart. Later I looked again, and this time, to my surprise, it appeared to resemble the left and right sides of the brain. And finally, to my amazement, I realized that, more than anything, the map seemed to me like a woman's reproductive organs – the broad horizontal river representing fallopian tubes, the stream as birth canal and vagina, and the lake and sea suggestive of ovaries. The Kingdom of Tenderness was located at the site of sexual union and eventual birth. So what was born? Courtly love perhaps, sophisticated love, love independent of marriage, love which brought together mind and heart, reason and passion, conceived and brought to life in and through a woman's body.

Now it's time to wander around the corner to 36 rue des Tournelles to see the exterior of Ninon de Lanclos's house, the home she lived in for forty-eight years, from 1657 to her death in 1705. It's small and modest, a sign of Ninon's commitment to financial freedom and independence.

Just a few doors down from Ninon's house I come to a bridal shop. This is no snooty rue Saint-Honoré boutique. Nor is it a daring young designer's *atelier*, increasingly common in the Marais district. I peer in the dusty window. A puffy white wedding gown fills the grey space. As I look at it, I can't help but conjure the young woman who will buy this flouncing frock. I imagine her to be a conventional type, for whom the wedding day is an expression of social status as much as a ceremony of love. Nothing courtly or sophisticated, I smugly conclude, about *this* bourgeois love affair.

But if I were to be honest – if I were to apply to myself the ruthless standard of truth that the salonnières liked to apply to each other – this is not the only thought that runs through my mind. I must admit that the wedding dress indicates a certain sense of purpose that I most definitely lack. Matrimonial closure isn't my strong point. I seem to have spent most of my adult life passionately in love with someone or other, consumed by the idea of exalted romance, but paradoxically too distracted or disorganized to make any relationship succeed, let alone proceed to marriage. I could list many grand gestures I've made in the name of romance: costly visits to lovers in Iran or Mexico; exaggerated enthusiasms for hobbies (New York underground! Zen Buddhism! Surfing!) that secretly bored me; embarrassing scenes of self-abasement when relationships turned rocky; bleary red-eyed despair when they finally ended. But now I can hardly remember most of those men who once seemed so singular and essential to my happiness; in my mind they've become interchangeable, versions of each other. I discover, with a twinge of shame, that they were mostly bit players in my own personal drama. And there was nothing courtly or sophisticated about my romances, either.

I suspect if Ninon de Lanclos were around she might have a few thoughts on this. Curious to consider that, so long ago, certain women were far more sophisticated about human relations than we pride ourselves on being today. Ninon would surely mock the social competitiveness of the modern middle-class bride – after all, she herself eschewed ostentation and excess. But she might equally laugh at the over-inflated sagas of the modern romantic – at someone like me. Ninon would never be so shallow as to judge the success of a romance by the length of its duration. Nor would she condemn a woman for her many abbreviated – others might say, failed – relationships. On the contrary, three hundred years and a universe of

worldly wisdom away, she would remind me with sly and
elegant lasciviousness: *The woman who has loved but one*
man will never know love . . .

❦ 4 ❧

The Academy

One day the Abbé de Châteauneuf discovered [La
Maréchale de Grancey] all red with indignation. 'What
is the trouble, madam?' said he. 'I opened by hazard,' she
replied, 'a book which was lying about in my cabinet; it
is, I believe, a certain collection of letters. Therein I saw
these words: *Wives, submit yourselves unto your husbands.*
I threw the book away.'

                                                    Voltaire

CROSSING THE PONT DES ARTS, I am wondering
whether I could possibly feel any worse. The weather is
too warm. The sky is too bright. My clothes are too heavy
for this balmy day and my feet are already swelling. I'm
uncomfortable, and, it surprises me to detect, I'm nervous.

I look across to my destination, the Institut de France,
which rises in classical austerity above the Seine on the
Left Bank. Louis XIV's first prime minister, Cardinal
Mazarin, commissioned the building as a finishing school
for provincial French aristocrats. It was designed by the
great architect Le Vau and completed in 1688. In 1805,

Napoleon decided it would become the Institut de France, the home of the various French Académies of science and culture. The gilded white cupola of Cardinal Mazarin's chapel now looms over the ceremonial meetings of France's most prestigious academy, l'Académie Française. The Académie's task is to protect the French language, and, by extension, French culture. This is a sacred site in France. No wonder I feel nervous.

I'm also ill-prepared. To do anything in Paris one generally requires several letters of introduction, preferably with credentials, stamps and other visual symbols of importance, all supplied well in advance, because spontaneity does not sit well with the French. But I'm an Australian, I'm here for a short time, and I'm hopeful. I just wish I looked more elegant.

I walk slowly through the courtyard and up the stairs to be stopped by a soft-eyed, soft-bellied official. I inquire, cautiously, if there are to be any guided tours of the Institut. He nods, bored, eyes turned down.

'Yes, on the first Saturday of each month, Madame. We had a tour last Saturday, if Madame would like to register for the next one?'

I try to remain dignified, and fail. 'Oh, but I have to be back home by then. And it will be a while before I can get back here.' Just as I feared, here it comes: the look, the shrug, the indifferent silence.

'Perhaps I could write a letter? To gain entry on another occasion.' An upward curve of the lips is my answer: sure, it suggests, go right ahead.

'The thing is,' I say, 'I am looking for someone.'

'Oui, Madame?'

'Well, um, you see, it's possible that she is entombed under your cupola.'

Monsieur may be a mere guard at the Institut de France, but he is also a custodian of French culture. I watch the interest rise like a fast tide in his brown eyes. I can practically hear him upgrade me mentally from tourist (of no interest) to scholar (of potential value to the continuing glory of France).

Not that we rush into things. Monsieur slowly takes a generous breath and blows his nose. Then he leans into me, resting his belly comfortably against the counter. It's the cue for me to begin. And I tell him in my halting French the strange tale of Hortense Mancini, the most beautiful and wild of the five nieces of Cardinal Mazarin.

Hortense Mancini, Duchess of Mazarin, was just twenty-three years old in 1668 when she set off to pursue her fortune. She left her husband and four children, her palace and status, her security and honor. She never lived in France again. For the next seven years she roamed around Europe. For several years she settled as the mistress of the Duke of Savoy but when he died his widow, not unreasonably, threw Hortense out. Finally, Hortense rode into London in 1675, where she became one of the mistresses of merry King Charles II. She stayed in England for the rest of her life and died in London in 1699.

I stop to draw breath, but Monsieur decides to take charge of the conversation.

'Madame, if she died in London, why would you imagine that she is buried here in Paris?'

'Well, her husband remained obsessed with her for twenty years. He even mounted a lawsuit in England to force her to return to him. After she died, he came to England, put the body of Hortense in a coffin and carted it about Europe from one estate to another for many years. Hortense was carried from Vincennes to Brittany, from Bourbon to Alsace.'

'And then?' Monsieur's left eyebrow arches.

'What finally happened isn't clear. But according to the books I have read, it seems that Hortense was eventually buried in the sarcophagus with her uncle, Cardinal Mazarin.'

Monsieur nods slowly. But he doubles back to the question that no doubt has been troubling this Parisian from the start. 'Why on earth would she want to leave Paris in the first place?'

I have a very satisfactory answer to that one.

'Because her husband was mad,' I reply.

Monsieur nods with world-weary resignation: ah, yes, madness. He pauses for a beat. Then suddenly he draws back and looks over my shoulder at the clock on the wall behind me. He twists around to a wooden shelf hung with sets of keys. He plucks a handful from the shelf. 'Come on,' he says. 'But we must hurry.' But we don't hurry. We walk slowly across the courtyard. Monsieur uses his shoulders to coax his stomach to a forward momentum.

We walk up wide wooden stairs and now Monsieur unlocks a heavy door, ushering me into a high, greenish room. It's Cardinal Mazarin's chapel, the home of the Académie Française. The milky light from the cupola pours in. Forty green seats are arranged in a forest-colored semi-circle, like a mini parliament. There's a statue of Napoleon in one corner. It's cool here, and quiet, and very empty. Monsieur's chest swells with pride at this place, and its significance. Of course it does. Here some of the greatest have taken their place: Victor Hugo and Alfred de Musset, Chateaubriand and Jean Cocteau. I feel suitably, sincerely, awed.

And there, in an alcove, is a tomb. We walk over together, a little self-conscious now, and we stare at it. It consists of a large black sarcophagus on a pedestal. Standing upon it is Cardinal Mazarin himself in huge marble effigy, complete with pointy nose, flowing gowns and attendant cherub. Below the sarcophagus, guarding it perhaps, or advertising its importance, are three large carved ebony figures representing Peace, Prudence and Fidelity. This is a famous sculpture by Coysevox, but neither of us is thinking about this monument as a work of art. We are looking for the body.

We continue gazing intently at the tomb as if expecting Hortense to leap out from behind it. But even though the sarcophagus is clearly big enough for two, there is no sign whatsoever to indicate that Hortense Mancini has been buried with her uncle. No plaque, no statue, no nothing.

It occurs to me that, strictly speaking, Hortense was never welcome in this place. The Académie Française is famously a bastion of conservatism, and particularly sexism. Out of a total of seven hundred *Académiciens* since Cardinal Richelieu created the Académie in 1635, only four have been women. The first woman Académicien was Marguerite Yourcenar and she was elected in 1980, when she was seventy-seven years old. Even *she* was unsure of the legitimacy of her being there.

This uncertain, floating me, whose existence I myself dispute, Yourcenar said in her inaugural address to the assembly, *here it is, surrounded, accompanied by an invisible troupe of women who perhaps should have received this honour long before, so that I am tempted to stand aside to let their shadows pass . . .* Among the invisible troupe she mentioned were Germaine de Staël, George Sand and

Colette, not one of whom was ever invited to take their place in this room.

Yourcenar went on: *One cannot say that in French society, so impregnated with feminine influences, the Academy has been a notable misogynist; it simply conformed to the custom that willingly placed a woman on a pedestal but did not permit itself to officially offer her a chair.*

That, I think, was Hortense's situation. She was offered no formal 'chair'; indeed, she never produced a single work of art. But she did find herself upon a pedestal. Within a year of her arrival in London, Hortense was hosting an important salon, bringing the spirit of France into London society. As a contemporary noted, *All manner of subjects were discoursed upon there, as philosophy, history, pieces of wit and gallantry, plays, authors ancient and modern, the niceties of the French tongue and so on.* One of her courtiers was Ninon de Lanclos's pen friend, St Evremond, who faithfully attended her until she died. Hortense soon became one of Louis XIV's great exports, part of the marketing of French culture that occurred through the seventeenth century. Her political importance was such that the French Ambassador used to report to Louis XIV on Hortense's activities.

But now Monsieur is looking at me with narrowed eyes. 'She is not here,' he says, shaking his head at his own credulousness. He lifts his arm pointedly and looks at his watch.

Oh, yes, *I'm* not meant to be here either.

As I turn I think: of course, this is a place of male ritual. And even though this room is officially a center of French culture, of Frenchness, the absence of women makes it, in truth, un-French, even anti-French. This empty room is wonderful, but it's not where the heart of French culture beats. If it exists, it's surely somewhere else – it's where the women are. And if she were ever here, the presence of Hortense Mancini has now been completely erased.

We leave and the great key turns again in the lock. I sense that my guide wants to get rid of me quickly now that our quest has failed.

On the way downstairs, I thank Monsieur profusely, I apologize for disturbing him, and then, suddenly, regretfully, I am expelled from the cool fish tank of the Institut into the hot bright day. Instantly the sweat breaks out again on my legs. I need a surge of cold air and a drink.

⚜

Paris is one of the few cities in the world where a woman can be comfortable on her own. Solitary women are everywhere: in little teashops or brasseries, in bistros or restaurants. Sometimes women bring a docile husband with them (whom they tend to ignore) or a little and ugly dog (which they lavishly pet). Now I notice a new accessory has taken off – the mobile phone.

But there are still plenty of women like me, cheerfully alone, cooling down in a modest teashop behind the Louvre. During earlier visits to Paris I liked to pose in café windows looking moody and intellectual, scribbling into a notebook what I fondly told myself were haunting haiku. Now I don't bother. I don't bother to look purposeful and get out a mobile phone or a diary and write. I do what Parisians do – I sit and stare.

Have you ever wondered at the numbers of mirrors in Paris? I used to think it was because Parisians were vain and liked to look at themselves. But it's not that, or not only that. It's because the French enjoy looking at people, and don't mind being looked at in return. It's why the most famous reception room in France is the Hall of Mirrors in Versailles. It's why all the café chairs are side by side and face the streets. Inside many cafés a mirrored strip around the wall ensures that each face is seen from three angles. The French are comfortable with the provocative idea that other people make interesting viewing. (The writer Colette's very last words were *Regarde! Regarde!*) This is a profoundly disturbing notion to Anglo-Celtic societies, which is one reason I like it so much. I also like it because of its next logical conclusion: if people are objects of aesthetic pleasure, then everyone has their role to play in contributing to the beauty of their surroundings.

That's one reason why visiting the Hall of Mirrors is always a faintly disappointing experience – the mirrors should reflect exquisite men and women twirling in ice-cream-colored silks and snowy wigs under the warm twinkle of thousands of candles. Instead, they reflect Midwestern Americans in primary colored microfibers.

As I sip my drink, my head is framed in triplicate for anyone who cares to look at me. I am reminded of that famous Brassai photograph of the thirties' lovers caught multiply in corner mirrors, she with her head arched playfully back and her cigarette raised; he leaning in to her, captivated; and we, Brassai's curious audience, peering at both.

Which gets me thinking about Hortense again. She was one of those women people looked at – and talked about – all her life. There's a portrait of Hortense with one delicate breast exposed in a white chemise. She gazes serenely at the viewer – she might, you imagine, be surprised if she looked down and caught sight of her vagrant nipple. Or perhaps not, for Hortense took to the life of a courtesan with remarkable gusto.

Hortense Mancini grew up in the spotlight, a European celebrity from birth. She was the second youngest of Cardinal Mazarin's five Mancini nieces – Parisians called them *Les Mazarinettes* – each of them brought over from Italy as children. Courtesan Ninon de Lanclos wrote to St Evremond that she thought charm ran through their blood. But even among this bevy of beauties, Hortense was special. Not only was she the most beautiful of the Cardinal's nieces, she was one of the most perfect beauties of Louis XIV's young court. She had pale olive skin, large blue-grey eyes, soft black curls and a statuesque figure. One contemporary admirer said she wasn't like one of those insipid French dolls, but more of a 'lofty Roman Beauty'. Even when she was getting older, Hortense retained her powerful appeal: at the age of thirty-nine, men were still fighting duels over her. As Madame de Sévigné exclaimed, *Who would have believed that the eyes of a grandmother could work such havoc?*

Hortense's beauty alone doesn't explain why she fascinated so many people. She was famous because she broke the rules. People in court circles felt that vicarious shiver of excitement as they followed the next instalment of the Hortense Mancini story: what would she do next? It wasn't that Hortense set out to destroy society or undermine its values. She wasn't a romantic rebel or social revolutionary; far from it. She simply wanted to redefine her own place within society, to re-establish the social order under different circumstances. But that alone, of course, was daring enough.

When her protector, the Duke of Savoy, died in 1675 and Hortense was forced to seek shelter in England, she couldn't travel from northern Italy across France because her obsessive husband still had spies looking out for her. Hortense had to ride across French enemy territory in Switzerland, Alsace and Germany to Amsterdam to embark on the boat for England. She dressed as a man in the wig, plumed hat and silk culottes of a cavalier. She had abandoned her past and faced an uncertain future, but you wouldn't have guessed it. On the way she bumped into a girlfriend who, far from delighting in her friend's good spirits, was outraged that Hortense refused to be humbled by life's disasters. *What is most strange*, railed Sidonie de Courcelles, *is that this woman triumphs over all her misfortunes by an excess of folly which has no parallel and that after receiving this setback she thinks only of enjoying herself. When passing through here she was on horseback, befeathered and bewigged, escorted by twenty men. She talked of nothing but violins and of hunting parties and everything else that gives pleasure.*

This story, of course, made the rounds of the Paris salons. Depending on their temperament, Parisians were either captivated or appalled by a woman who seemed so happy in the midst of her life's shambles.

While Hortense was King Charles II's mistress, one of his daughters, by his long-standing mistress Barbara Cleveland, fell passionately in love with her. Instead of carefully discouraging this inappropriate relationship, Hortense ignored the King's explicit instructions and therefore her own clear social and financial interests. She and the Countess of Sussex struck up a scandalous friendship: they even took up fencing together, according to one outraged observer, dashing boisterously into St James Park for early-morning jousts with drawn swords beneath their nightgowns. It was typical of Hortense to follow her instincts rather than her interests. As a result, the King downgraded his relationship with her immediately. Hortense became less important to ambassadors; her income less secure; her social status only guaranteed by her own charms, not her royal associations. Yet in London her salon continued to shine.

For Hortense, life was irrepressibly about *everything that gives pleasure*. The puritans and the naysayers couldn't bear it that Hortense broke the rules and got away with it. They used words like *folly* and *dissoluteness* about her actions. The English puritan John Evelyn called her *that famous and errant Lady, the Dutchesse of Mazarine*, adding darkly, *all the world knows her storie*. But Hortense's pursuit of pleasure wasn't dissolute: it was so arrow-like, so direct and unalloyed, it attained almost to innocence.

I decide to ignore my tiredness and walk the short distance to see where her adventures began – and to contemplate all that she left behind.

The Bibliothèque Richelieu on rue de Richelieu was formerly the national library of France, but now houses some of the nation's specialist manuscript and coin collections. I pause on the street outside to read the plaque. At the center of this complex of palaces and grand houses is the Palais Mazarin, formerly the Hôtel Tubeuf, owned by Cardinal Mazarin and bequeathed to his sixteen-year-old niece Hortense on the occasion of her marriage. I feel a pleased tingle. Here was Hortense Mancini's home for seven years.

I walk through the courtyard and then wind my way around the library foyer, poking my head down corridors and into various reading rooms. I'm looking for one particular room but don't really expect to find it – numerous renovations will surely have submerged it or altered it beyond recognition. But this is Paris, and of course I should know better. For, unexpectedly, here I am. I recognize it instantly from the descriptions I have read. The gallery is long and wide. The high ceiling is elaborately painted. Grand alcoves form natural display cases, backlit by arched windows. And here's the bust of the Cardinal himself, sitting high over the portal. It's as if I have dropped into Hortense's life at that decisive moment, when the event took place that would trigger her vagabond wanderings. I look around expectantly, but it's clear that these scholarly and preoccupied French people do not share my excitement.

When Cardinal Mazarin bequeathed his home to his niece and her husband, he also left them his priceless collection of classical sculptures, carefully selected and installed in a long gallery built for the purpose. This room. The collection of Greek and Roman antiquities was famous – it was certainly the most important of its kind in France, and one of the greatest in Europe. These were peerless objects of beauty, representing a pinnacle of aesthetic achievement and a monument to the enlightenment of the ancient world.

But, as I explained to Monsieur at the Institut, Hortense Mancini's husband, the duc de Mazarin, was mad. His insanity had a prudish, religious edge to it. He wanted his little daughters to have their front teeth extracted so they wouldn't be dangerously beautiful like their mother. He wouldn't let the women of his household staff look at cows being milked as he was sure it provoked lewd thoughts. No one liked him: even the King, Louis XIV himself, couldn't stand him. No wonder. The duc used to lecture the King on his infidelities, saying he was instructed to do so by the Archangel Gabriel.

One warm night in June 1668, the duc walked into this

room. He looked around at the four hundred classical statues, the vast majority of which were, of course, nude. He was offended; more than this, he was appalled. He called for a hammer and began slowly, methodically, madly smashing the statues. It took a long time. The King learned of the desecration and sent emissaries to try and stop the tragedy, but it was too late. A priceless collection of antiquities had been destroyed.

This was the event that triggered Hortense's flight from her husband. Soon after, she put on men's clothes, collected her jewels, packed up her bags and left on horseback. Her distraught husband woke Louis XIV at 3 am to tell him the news. But by then the King had lost patience with this proselytizing bore. *'And why did the Archangel Gabriel not give you warning?'* the monarch asked irritably.

Hortense simply walked out on her own life. She left behind wealth, privilege and a social position at the heart of French society. Not to mention four young children. Given all the more immediate and personal causes her husband had given her to leave, it seems to me both striking and appropriate that an act of aesthetic destruction triggered Hortense's flight. For some reason, this impersonal attack on beauty was, for her, the final blow to her marriage. Thereafter she was ardent in pursuit of the beauty and pleasure her husband had sought to destroy.

I wander through the library a little longer, and then head for the nearby Galerie Colbert, a gorgeous nineteenth-century arcade or *passage*, where the library has a small bookshop. As I stroll I have to admit to myself that, though I like to dwell on Hortense's glorious escape to freedom, this is, of course, not the whole of her story.

As for so many women, life got harder for Hortense as she got older. With the death of Charles II, she became vulnerable. She had money worries. Her husband kept pursuing and tormenting her. She never formed a stable romantic relationship, though she still had many friends and admirers who thronged her salon. She took to drinking a little too much. Even her epicurean capacity to live in an eternal present failed her at one stage. She hung her apartments in black and thought about going to Spain and entering a convent with her sister Marie. St Evremond wrote her a long letter explaining that such extreme options were suitable for the ugly and foolish only: *When* [they] *throw themselves into nunneries, it is a divine inspiration.* He urged Hortense to remember her assets: *You were brought up as a Queen and you deserved to be one.*

I can imagine Hortense nodding and smiling at this. And obviously her natural optimism reasserted itself, for in 1696, at the age of fifty-one and just three years before her death, Hortense wrote to St Evremond simply: *Never was I in better health; never was I handsomer in all my life.*

A few hours ago, back at the Institut de France, as we strolled across the courtyard to the chapel in the other wing, Monsieur looked at me and asked rather a disconcerting question: 'Why are you interested in Hortense Mancini?'

I could have replied with the predictable caveats. I could have said that I admired Hortense because, even though she was really rather shallow and terribly vain and absolutely foolhardy, well, she was very brave. But that would not have been quite true. The truth is that Hortense's shallowness, her vanity and her foolhardiness were essential to her courage. These were the very character traits that gave her the

capacity to escape. A more thoughtful woman, an intro-
vert, a worrier, a sensitive soul, simply could not have
made the wild break for freedom that Hortense did.
And survive. And flourish. It was far too difficult to
explain that I didn't admire her in spite of her faults:
I admired her because of them. So I smiled and tried to
look scholarly. 'She was an important Frenchwoman,'
I said. Monsieur nodded. At the Institut de France, the
guards understand that kind of thing.

Now I am truly exhausted. I head off home, via rue de
Bretagne. I buy salad leaves and melting cheeses and bread
and wine and some headily fragrant strawberries and
devour a solitary spring feast as I pore over an old map.
Then I fall into bed and dream of airports with high
painted ceilings and airport queues lined with broken
statues and in the midst of it all a baby girl with a wisp of
dark hair and luminous eyes, gazing at her future.

⤟ 5 ⤞

Le Grand Véfour

Paris is a great beauty. As such it possesses all the qualities
that one finds in any other great beauty; chic, sexiness,
grandeur, arrogance, and the absolute inability and refusal
to listen to reason.

Fran Lebowitz

LIKE A BLAST of fresh air, Rachel is back. She looks fan-
tastic: her severe suit and stark jewelry set off her white
skin, diamond-shaped green eyes and fine curling hair.
Rachel is smart, really smart. She can be intimidating. She
doesn't walk, she stalks. She rarely smiles, though she often
laughs. She's also one of the most generous and thoughtful people I have ever met.

We rapidly consume a bottle of champagne and then
take ourselves to a tiny little restaurant around the
corner called Chez Nenesse. On Rachel's instruction
I order the onion soup. She swears it will be the best I've

ever had. She's right, it's delicious – a murky, rich, stringy broth.

'I'm going to take a few days off,' Rachel says. 'Wander around with you as you look for your girls.'

My first instinct is doubt. Rachel has possibly the lowest boredom threshold of anyone I know. 'It could be incredibly tedious,' I warn. 'The other day I spent the morning looking for the non-existent tomb of Hortense Mancini. This whole trip could be spent looking for things that don't exist.'

'That's OK. You need me anyway. I have a sense of direction.'

True.

'Plus,' Rachel went on, 'I need a rest. My heart beats too fast. I'm not sleeping well. It'll be good for me just to lope around with you. If I get bored I'll come home or do a few practical things like getting the dry-cleaning done or shoe repairs.'

I am a little surprised. 'Is Paris wearing you down? To me, of course, it always looks as though this is the one perfectly civilized place left in the world.'

Rachel snorts. 'Civilized? French women are completely neurotic; they're all on several kinds of pills. And even though they won't do any exercise, they are obsessed with their weight – they starve themselves. They smoke to suppress their appetites.' She pauses and looks at her own cigarette. 'Whereas I smoke because I'm addicted.'

I look down at a soupspoon full of cheesy melting bread. 'So you mean my current diet of three enormous French meals a day isn't going to make me lean and lithe?'

Rachel ignores me. 'I've heard of doctors telling perfectly normal pregnant women to cut back their food intake because they were putting on too much weight. I tell you they're obsessive about it.'

This is all a bit lowering.'The story goes that the French live wonderfully sane lives. And that French women are beautiful because they eat a balanced diet and go to the seaside for two months a year and invest carefully in nice underwear, shoes and bags . . .

'. . . And plastic surgery and the rest,' Rachel adds.'The effort is not so obvious because French women don't walk around in track-pants like Americans do and tell everyone how hungry they are and how often they go to the gym.' Rachel stabs out her cigarette.'Which we have to admit is a great blessing.

'I mean, they do spend a fortune on grooming. It's why I took to doing my nails – I couldn't get any respect otherwise.' She holds up her white hands tipped with very un-French blood plum nail polish. They look great.

Rachel pauses.'Still, they have the best shoe shop in the world, Robert Clergerie. And Paris may be a museum theme park, but it's beautiful. And at their best, French restaurants are *the* best.'

'Good,' I say, 'because I've reserved lunch for us tomorrow at Grand Véfour.'

Later that night, I lie in bed as a ray of blond moonlight streams into my room. Rachel is right. Paris is not a relaxed city. Standards are high. It is not that French women are glamorous; in fact, they tend to be understated in appearance. Their clothes are conservative. Heels are not usually high. They are exceptionally well groomed, but in a subtle way. It looks effortless, but of course it isn't. And it's damned hard to copy. *Beauty without grace is a hook without bait*, said Ninon de Lanclos. They seem to have found grace.

Way back in 1804, the American writer Washington Irving wrote home to his brothers: *If the ladies of France have not handsome faces given them by nature, they have the art of improving them vastly, and setting nature at defiance. Besides, they never grow old: you stare perhaps, but I assure you it is a fact.* I can imagine Irving's brothers reading this, looking across their austere living rooms to their faded American brides, and sighing with repressed regret for these age-less Gallic sirens. Irving added passionately that French women, *set fire to the head and set fire to the tail.*

I once asked Ellen what she thought about French women.

'Yes, I like them very much,' she said.

'But don't some people find them, you know, uptight and competitive?'

'Oh, they are,' she said. 'But you know,' she added, in that low sinuous way of hers, 'I'm a bit like that myself. I'm more of a man's woman.'

She looked at me with her knowing smile. 'They play games, you know? They're complex and interesting. And they're not *girly*,' she concluded with satisfaction.

It only occurred to me later that Ellen had used the word *girly* as an insult.

As I drift off to sleep a last, fleeting thought: I'm fairly sure no one has ever observed that Australian women set men on fire.

⚜

It's a fresh clear day and Rachel and I are all high-heeled and dark nail-polished and shiny-haired. We climb out of our taxi, strut along the arcades of the Palais Royal and present ourselves at the wood and glass doors of Le Grand Véfour, one of the oldest and best restaurants in Paris. It seems the entire lunch sitting has arrived together. There's a gratifying whooshing and whirring as we are guided to our table and ushered along the cherry velvet banquettes and large menus are flipped open and corks are pulled and popped. With floor-to-ceiling murals of classical maidens and curling vines and bowls of fruit, Le Grand Véfour is less like a restaurant and more like an intimate salon.

In our sharp suits, Rachel and I are rather ill-matched to this ridiculously pretty and convivial room. I can't help thinking that we should be dressed to suit the late eighteenth-century days when those doors first opened. Women's fashions were sexy – very low-cut, high-waisted, ultra-sheer gowns set off by lace-up sandals revealing ankles and legs. Hair was often short and curled around the face, goddess-style, and cameos were popular as jewelry. Fashionable women revived this Hellenic style to signal a renewed hope in the Revolution. Paris, the optimists hoped, would be the new Athens – democratic, open and sophisticated.

But instead of becoming a noble Athenian democracy, Paris degenerated into a frontier town. The city was flooded with a strange brew of *émigré* aristocrats, army contractors, black marketeers, revolutionaries and speculators. Spiralling inflation and a downgraded currency produced great bargains for those with foreign cash. It was a time for people on the make. Political power was in the hands of a corrupt and opportunistic Directory of five men. At the head of the Directory was one Paul Barras. His mistress was a thirty-something widow with two children. Her name was Rose de Beauharnais. One day she would become Napoleon's Josephine and the Empress of France.

Rose de Beauharnais was all woman. Her teeth may have rotted from the cane sugar of her native Caribbean

island, but with her soft voice and languid walk, tilted
nose and curling eyelashes, she was intensely, marvelously
feminine. Much like this room, in fact, where she regularly
dined. Perhaps she sat right here, sipping champagne. In
her position of influence, she was able to scam some
money herself, by petitioning and trading on arms con-
tracts. It helped her pay the debts to her dressmakers.

Our waiter now approaches. He inclines his sleek head
gravely. 'An apéritif, Mesdames?'

We hesitate. 'Well, we would like a glass of champagne
to start and, what do you think? We were thinking of
drinking champagne right throughout our meal.' An
approving nod, a smile.

'*Certainement*, Mesdames,' he responds. 'Perfectly proper,
and may I suggest the Deutz.'

He recommends the daily *menu fixe*; we accept. He
pours our first champagne; we sip. He brings us the first
of a sequence of delicious dishes; we tuck in. We are
enjoying the rare pleasure of passivity, for we are in the
hands of experts.

One dish I will always remember. I think it may be a
work of art, or philosophy. Three mouthfuls are carefully
dispersed on Limoges china: a tomato sorbet, a tomato
mousse and a tomato terrine. Three colors, and, on the
tasting, three textures. Each mouthful reveals a slightly different aspect of the fruit – here's the sweetness, then the
slight zing and finally, the warm basenote. It's a discourse
on tomatoness, both subtle and exquisite. And swiftly
gone.

Every now and then passersby, on their stroll around
the arcades of the Palais Royal, stop and peer through the
lace-covered windows. They want to see this famous
room, and I can understand why: I've done it myself. Now

that I'm inside, of course, I'm trying not to look at them looking in at me.

In the heady summer of 1795, many more visitors wandered the Palais Royal looking for entertainments both pure and impure. Paris was in the grip of an extended, dissolute, after-the-Terror party. The excesses of the guillotine were over. The fanatic Robespierre was dead. People no longer needed to look fearfully over their shoulders. Instead they overcame the horror of recent deaths by an exuberant embrace of life. Women danced with narrow red ribbons around their necks to symbolize the severed head.

Amid this excess, the Palais Royal was the headquarters of pleasure. All the cafés, restaurants, theaters, brothels and gambling houses were filled to bursting. But there was a lonely figure among the revelers. He was an obscure young soldier named Napoleon Buonaparte, newly arrived in Paris from the provinces. At twenty-six years of age, he was pale, intense and silent, but even then he was an acknowledged genius on the battlefield. Born in Corsica, Napoleon was essentially Italian; he was as tough, clannish and ruthless as a mafia godson.

This macho soldier, obsessed with the acquisition and exercise of power, was understandably surprised when he figured out the real sources of power in Directory Paris. He wrote home to his brother Joseph:

Women are everywhere – applauding the plays, reading in the bookshops, walking in the Park. The lovely creatures even penetrate to the professor's study. Paris is the only place in the world where they deserve to steer the ship of state; the men are mad about them, think of nothing else, only live by them and for them. Give a woman six months in Paris, and she knows where her empire is, and what is her due.

When Napoleon met Rose de Beauharnais he confronted the apogee of this new woman: she was graceful,
untruthful, influential, extravagant and amoral. She was as
unlike his thrifty, virtuous, domineering mother as it was
possible to be. But her very faults made her *une vraie
femme*, the very essence of femininity, her charms as
delicate as gossamer.

From their first night together Napoleon was utterly
infatuated with the elegant, alluring older woman, whom
he possessively renamed Josephine:

> *I awake all filled with you. Your image, and the intoxicating pleasures
> of last night, allow my senses no rest. Sweet and matchless Josephine,
> how strangely you work upon my heart! . . . a thousand kisses, mio
> dolce amor; but give me none back, for they set my blood on fire.*

As I gaze around this restaurant, it seems to me that
feminine style still holds a special place in Paris. On the
other side of the room is a table of imposing old men,
lawyers or judges perhaps, chewing their food lustily.
Perhaps it's their monthly lunch. They are having a wonderful time. To Australian eyes it's noteworthy: a group of
powerful men choosing to dine in an atmosphere as
feminine as a beauty parlor.

In Sydney, Rachel and I agree, there is no way a group
of men lunching together would ever consent to eat in a
room as pretty as this. They would feel emasculated by
their surroundings. 'Even gay men,' I suggest to Rachel,
'tend to prefer leather and stainless steel.'

At another table, absorbed in their own drama, are an
American man and a much younger woman. He is suited,
she is casually dressed, and her long legs are curling ner-
vously around the legs of her chair. He keeps talking, staring

at her intently. She looks distractedly away, flicking her long hair. I think: how curious, he finds this restaurant romantic and hopes its charms will seduce her (as he intends to); she merely finds it old-fashioned and is bored witless.

Rachel and I feel right at home. Glowing with champagne and fine food, caressingly administered to by our waiter, we are the last to leave, outstaying even the lawyers. The oldest is so infirm he has to be carried out by his colleagues, still waving his post-prandial cigar. Five hours after our arrival Rachel and I finally stumble out into the pale pink afternoon, blinking with woozy pleasure. 'Now that,' she says, 'was a lunch.'

⚜

Next morning, as I peer out the downstairs window onto a drizzly sidewalk, Rachel's voice rings out like a commandment behind me: 'So where are we off to today?'

'Well, I was thinking of looking for the place where Napoleon and Josephine got married, and checking to see whether Josephine's cottage is still there . . .'

'Right. When do we start?'

'. . . and really I am not sure whether I have the right addresses, because that part of Paris changed so much under the redesign of Baron Haussmann, and even the street numbers could have changed and it's all a bit of guesswork but oh well if you really want to come . . .'

So off we go, taking the Métro from Filles du Calvaire to Opéra and winding our way down to rue d'Antin. On this cool wet day, the boulevards – once the legendary thoroughfares of carefree *boulevardiers* and *flâneurs* – are charmless, big, loud and impersonal. I can see that Rachel is already wondering what she's doing here as she struggles with her umbrella.

Rue d'Antin offers no compensation; it's as drab and grey as the day. We count our way along the street to find number 3, which was once the local town hall but is now a rather plain-looking bank branch. It doesn't matter to me. I feel childishly triumphant when I see a plaque; it's as welcome as a personal greeting. Lucinda, it trumpets, you've come to the right place.

Translated the plaque says:

1796–1996
Commemoration of the marriage of
Napoleon Bonaparte
and
Josephine de Beauharnais
9 March 1996, Napoleon Foundation

This gold print on white marble bestows posthumous dignity on what was, in fact, a very odd occasion. The bride was thirty-three years old and wasn't at all certain about this strange match she had reluctantly agreed to make. She had plenty of time to think about her decision: the groom was three hours late. When the twenty-seven-year-old hero Bonaparte bustled in, he shook the dozing registrar awake and the couple were united in a two-minute ceremony, following which they climbed into a carriage and rode to Josephine's rented cottage in rue Chantereine. There, on their wedding night, Napoleon gave Josephine a gold locket on a chain inscribed *To Destiny* and Josephine's jealous pug, Fortuné, nipped the bridegroom on the leg. Just two days later Napoleon went to command the French forces in Italy.

I'm gazing at the plaque and passing enjoyable moments wondering why it is dated 9 March and not

6 March, which is the date of the wedding according to my favorite work on this subject, *Napoleon and Josephine* by Evangeline Bruce. Why the discrepancy? I wonder. I smile at myself: I make an unlikely scholar. Then I look at Rachel's face, which is a mask of boredom. Mmm, perhaps we'll move along.

Rachel takes charge of the map and guides us on the short walk to rue de la Victoire, formerly rue Chantereine, to the site of Josephine's little cottage and the couple's first marital home. Oh dear. If rue d'Antin was disappointing, this is far worse. It's a shabby street and all we find at number 6 is a decidedly sleazy-looking sauna next to a rundown gym, neither of which appear to have any patrons. 'Are you sure this is the right place?' asks Rachel, none too subtly, as the drizzle turns to an outright downpour.

I look around from under my drumming umbrella, hoping for a plaque or a sign, anything to suggest that this was once the site of Josephine's charming little cottage where she was said to have all the luxuries and none of the necessities. Meanwhile Rachel's foot is tapping impatiently under her black umbrella and I observe her nervy hand fumbling for a cigarette in her handbag. It's true there's nothing of interest to see here now, nothing at all.

But as I look down the street, the past easily slides over the present. Twice a day Napoleon's envoys would gallop along here to deliver messages affirming the little General's passionate devotion to his new wife. Here was possibly the greatest military genius in history conducting a major campaign, and yet, Parisians noted with wonder, Josephine received reports from the front even before Barras himself.

Napoleon wrote to his wife: *Not a day passes without my*

loving you, not a night but I hold you in my arms . . . Whether I am buried in business, or leading my troops, or inspecting the camps, my adorable Josephine fills my mind, takes up all my thoughts, and reigns alone in my heart . . .

And: *What art did you learn to captivate all my faculties, to absorb all my character into yourself? It is a devotion, dearest, which will end only with my life. 'He lived for Josephine': there is my epitaph. I strive to be near you: I am nearly dead with desire for your presence. It is madness!*

And then there were the erotic letters: *A kiss on your heart, and then another a little lower, much* much *lower.* And:

I am going to bed with my heart full of your adorable image . . . I cannot wait to give proofs of my ardent love. How happy I would be if I could assist at your undressing, the little firm white breast, the adorable face, the hair tied up in a scarf à la créole. You know that I never forget the little visit, you know, the little black forest . . . I kiss it a thousand times and wait impatiently for the moment I will be in it. To live within Josephine is to live in the Elysian fields. Kisses on your mouth, your eyes, your breast, everywhere, everywhere.

I was enthralled when I first read these letters – blown over by them, by their ardent and earthy passion, and blown over by *her*, this woman who could inspire such outsize emotion. But Josephine was no needy modern lover. Napoleon's burning letters would arrive – right here, where I am standing, in fact, or hereabouts – and she would absentmindedly put them to one side, to be read later: *Qu'il est drôle, Bonaparte!* she would murmur affectionately – *What a funny thing he is.* Often she forgot to read his letters at all. Her own letters to him were irregular, bland and brief, sending Napoleon into a frenzy: *I get only one letter from you every four days!* Once she forgetfully addressed her husband in the formal *vous* eliciting further howls of distress from the front.

And perhaps it is no wonder the neglectful Josephine was unmoved by her husband's long-distance ardor: she was preoccupied by a passionate affair with a handsome young officer. Napoleon was a hero to France, but just a clumsy suitor to his wife. As we turn to depart, I marvel at Josephine's careless power.

Rachel and I walk in single file along rue de la Victoire, crossing the street by which we entered. Ahead of me I see the sign of a little café, Café Chantereine. It's a reference to this street's original name. I nod and shrug: well, at least we came to the right street, even if there was nothing here. As I turn to suggest to Rachel that we stop at Café Chantereine for a commemorative coffee, my raised umbrella frames another sign still further along the road, a dirty old wooden shingle. Hôtel de Beauharnais, it reads.

On an impulse, I lead Rachel out of the rain and into the narrow dark hotel foyer. It's the grimy boarding house of a thousand down-at-the-heel travel tales. At the front desk to our left, a woman is sitting with a phone in one hand and a cigarette in the other. Engrossed in her conversation, she takes no notice of us, assuming, I suppose, that we are some of her budget residents.

But as our eyes adjust to the dingy surroundings, we behold a surprising sight. Opposite the landlady, framed hugely in gilt, is Josephine herself. It's an amateur copy of her famous Imperial portrait by Gérard. Even the rough paintwork cannot diminish the luminous subject. In her gold and white gown, Josephine's delicate face is framed by her dark curling hair. As she gazes out of the painting she is gentle and regal at the same time. The copyist's hand may be heavy, but he or she is alert to the delicate nuances of the original painting: the set of Josephine's mouth is tentative, even apprehensive, and her eyes are dark with dread. Josephine never wanted Napoleon to declare himself the Emperor of France because she knew what would follow. The Emperor would want to fulfil his dynastic ambitions. To do so, he would have to divorce Josephine who was by then past child-bearing age. The day Josephine became consort to an Emperor was the beginning of the end of her marriage. In this portrait, the newly crowned Empress Josephine is looking into her future, and what she sees is sadness.

In front of Josephine's portrait is a small table. It is covered with a lace cloth and a little cracked vase filled gently with roses, Josephine's signature flower. The composition reflects an impulse so private, so tender, that we are quite taken aback.

Rachel's green eyes shine like a cat's in the gloom; for her, this appalling wet trek around Paris has gained human interest. The Paris of the past has all at once connected with the city she lives in today.

'It's a . . .' I begin.

'I know, it's a . . .' says Rachel.

'It's a shrine,' we whisper with joy.

I look closely at the tired, tough-featured woman at the front desk. She seems an unlikely devotee of the fragrant Josephine. And yet, I am sure that she is Josephine's admirer; that she finds some rare beauty in the woman who once lived on this street.

I would like to approach the woman, to make some connection with her and ask her about the portrait and her touching devotional gesture but she doesn't choose to acknowledge us. She puts down the phone and instantly picks it up again, barking weary commands in hoarse French. So we leave.

'Wow,' sighs Rachel into the damp air.

'I know,' I reply.

If a vote were taken on the most popular queen in French history, Josephine might well win, for she was loving, lovable, beloved. She had a youthful spirit and a tender, wayward heart. At the age of thirty-three she captivated a hero. And through her grace as consort, she bewitched a nation. Her garden at Malmaison became an important scientific and horticultural center. She cultivated wildflowers from the newly discovered Australian continent. Black swans from Western Australia swam in her lake and emus ran through her forest. Her rose garden was recorded by Redouté in works of art as well as natural history. Napoleon is well known for his scientific and cultural interests, but his wife made her own major contribution to knowledge. Not bad for the daughter of a poor French settler in the West Indies, an indolent, dreamy girl, swinging on a hammock and rotting her teeth on sugar cane.

The rain recedes as we exit rue de la Victoire, street of the victory. Josephine's textbook femininity is outmoded these days: the modern woman is a substantive and explainable being, not an airy and elusive creature. In her day, however, though Napoleon was the warrior, Josephine's arsenal of emotional weaponry was equally powerful. Napoleon used to say, proudly, wonderingly, *I win battles . . . Josephine wins hearts.*

Napoleon divorced Josephine in 1809 in a formal, public ceremony. Josephine retained her famous, gentle dignity to the last. But her soon-to-be ex-husband wept openly. He sobbed, *God alone knows what this resolve has cost my heart . . .*

∾ 6 ∾

Courtesans

It should be remembered, too, that in the eighteenth century pleasure was not regarded with the cold disapproval of our dismal age.

Nancy Mitford

MANY COUNTRIES have a great house, a place that symbolizes the nation state in all its authority and power. There's the White House in Washington. There's Number 10 Downing Street in London. In Australia, far less grandly, there's the Lodge in Canberra. In Paris, of course, there's the Palais de l'Élysée, 55–57 rue du Faubourg Saint-Honoré, at the corner of Avenue de Marigny. This is the home of the French President.

But as I stand across the road, gazing at the immaculate guards and the high gates of the Élysée, I am not thinking about the grandeur of this place. I am thinking how delightful it is – how quintessentially French it is – that the French President should live in a home owned and decorated by a courtesan, the famous Madame de Pompadour, mistress to Louis XV and the most gifted woman of her age.

This house was designed purely for love and pleasure. I'm sure France is the only nation in the world to permit such a feminine, romantic – and let's face it, decadent – association to contaminate a position of national authority. Well, it could never happen in America. Or Australia. Which is not to say that, even in France, everyone was comfortable with the idea. When General de Gaulle became President for the second time in 1959, he resisted moving into the Élysée. Apparently he thought the romantic frescoes on the ceilings were decidedly un-statesmanlike. Not to mention the cherubs in the Presidential office.

I would give anything to tour the Élysée, but of course it is closed to the public and heavily protected. Sometimes I see President Chirac and world leaders on television, important men posing for the camera with their heavy frames perched awkwardly on dainty Pompadour couches.

Nancy Mitford introduced me to La Marquise de Pompadour through her biography, published in 1953. She wrote about Madame de Pompadour with such intimacy and affection, I felt as though I knew her myself. Critics said that Nancy Mitford had created Madame de Pompadour in her own image, which may explain my intense affection for both author and subject. When she finished writing her biography, Nancy wrote to Evelyn Waugh: *I have lost the poor Marquise . . . & I miss her fearfully, my constant companion for nearly a year.*

The 'poor Marquise' hosted her very last party in this house before she died of tuberculosis at Versailles in 1764, aged forty-five. But the ghost of Madame de Pompadour hovers gracefully not only over this wonderful house; she is the presiding genius of this whole area. With a mental nod to the Marquise, I am about to take a stroll down one of the loveliest streets in the world, a street whose keynote is femininity.

Madame de Pompadour loved beautiful things – music, ideas, clothes, paintings, household objects. A gifted, middle-class, sensible *Parisienne*, she would surely have become a salonnière had destiny not stepped in. When she was a little girl a fortune-teller told her she would be the great love of a king: teasingly, her family nicknamed her *Reinette*. The dream, remarkably, came true. King Louis XV fell in love with the charming *bourgeoise* and swept her off to Versailles. Together they pursued their shared passion – the art of graceful living.

La Pompadour became the tastemaker of her age. Hers was perhaps the only time in history that a young woman presided over a major art movement – the rococo – with unashamed femininity as its keynote. Like François Boucher's rosy breasts and bottoms, it was light, lavish and shamelessly decorative. This was not grand or monumental art, it was charming and domestic, art embedded in the details of everyday life.

A hundred years after Pompadour's death, the Goncourt brothers, journalists and critics, described it this way:

When Louis XV succeeded Louis XIV, when a gay, amorous society emerged from a ceremonious one, and when, in the more human atmosphere of the new court, the stature of persons and things diminished, the prevailing artistic ideal remained factitious and conventional but it was an ideal that had descended from the majestic to the charming. There was everywhere diffused refined

elegance, a delicate voluptuousness, what the epoch itself defined as
'the quintessence of the agreeable, the complexion of grace and
charm, the adornments of pleasure and love'.

Pompadour, the greatest mistress in history, was a specialist in creating *the adornments of pleasure*. Every
woman who has relished a perfectly cut perfume bottle,
or an exquisite gold box, or a vase of luminous and fragile beauty, enjoys the legacy of Madame de Pompadour's
aesthetic vision. Her personal collection was astounding: gold engraved snuff boxes, rock crystal perfume
bottles with jewelled stops, musical clocks, dainty
teacups, lacquered tabletops, candles of gold and en-
twined porcelain flowers, blue and gold dinner plates.
There's a Boucher portrait of Madame de Pompadour
en négligé, applying makeup at her dressing table. She
wears a pink ribboned wrap, there's a blue flower in her
hair, in her hand is her gold pot of rouge, on the table is
her gold box and powder puff and there's a cameo of
her lover Louis XV attached to her wrist with lace.
Here, you think, is a woman who understands that allure lies in the details.

Pompadour single-handedly created the French cult of
quotidian beauty. It's no wonder that France today is the
world's greatest maker and marketer of affordable luxury
goods, small items of glamor that make women feel
special. La Pompadour transmitted *l'art de vivre* through
beautifying the sweet, small details of daily life.

Today the weather is cool and cloudy, perfect for a
spring walk. I follow rue du Faubourg Saint-Honoré as it
winds and dips, and it's going to be good exercise because
I have to keep running back and forth across the road to
savor every exquisitely presented shop window. Each turn

brings another. The names on the canopies tell a story of craftsmanship as well as glamor – *parfumerie* Annick Goutal, beauty salon Guerlain, ultra-luxe emporium Hermès, couturier Yves Saint Laurent . . .

One of the shops stops me in my tracks. It's a *confiserie*, the sort of place you will only see in France, in Paris. The boxes alone look good enough to eat. There are melt-in-your-mouth *pâtes de fruit*, rich golden *abricots confits*, nutty *marrons glacés*. Everything is shiny, tasty, tempting. And the pleasure begins here, in the anticipation, to be followed by each sweet's signature smell and, at last, the climactic mouthful. There's a discipline as well. You can't eat too many of these sweets, or too often. If you did you would soon reach a horrible surfeit. They offer simple pleasures, perhaps, but represent complex experiences, created with utmost care.

Pompadour nurtured French craftsmanship. She revived the Gobelins carpet and furniture factory in Paris, restoring its reputation and commercial success. She was instrumental in setting up the famous porcelain factory at Sèvres. She once planted a winter garden of china blossoms scented with perfume – laughing with delight when her lover the King, deceived by the ruse, bent over to smell a flower.

Pompadour was not without her strenuous detractors. Philosopher Jean-Jacques Rousseau – the man who brought us 'the noble savage' – vehemently denounced the rococo and the high civilization it represented. *These throngs of ephemeral works*, he thundered, *which come to light every day, made only to amuse women and having neither strength nor depth, fly from the dressing table to the counter.*

These *ephemeral works* weren't, however, antithetical to the Enlightenment spirit of progress; they reflected it.

Pompadour's aesthetic vision was bound up in the values and virtues of reason, learning, tolerance and good humor. One of the many ironies of the French revolution is that the reformist temperament was nurtured and came to flower in the very heart of aristocratic France. Pompadour herself owned two telescopes, a globe and possibly a microscope. As well as scientific journals, her library numbered over 3,000 volumes covering poetry, history, geography, novels and philosophy. *Philosophe* Dr Quesnay was her physician, and she steadfastly supported Voltaire, the single greatest figure of the Enlightenment. Pompadour is believed to have written the entry on *rouge* in the *Encyclopédie*. It was widely claimed that Louis XV plotted the path of the Seven Years War on maps laid out in Madame de Pompadour's bedroom: critics said she used her *mouches*, or beauty spots, to mark out the key events.

Rousseau and others regarded the rococo purely in light of the decadence and despair caused by the excesses of the court. Diderot reserved particular venom for Pompadour's favorite artist. *Boucher's elegance*, he lectured, *his affectation, romantic gallantry, coquetry, facility, variety, brilliance, rouged flesh tones, and debauchery will captivate dandies, society women, young people, men of the world, and the whole crowd of those who are strangers to true taste, to truth, to right thinking, to the gravity of art.*

I like to ponder that term: *the gravity of art*. It's a perfectly valid idea, of course, but I'll take the levity of art every time. Diderot was right, however, about the French gift for *facility, variety, brilliance*. No one could walk down this street without being struck by the French gift for selling beauty.

Pompadour herself was a master at image-making – and

image renewal. The early portraits portray the glamorous mistress, at her toilette or in a leafy bower. The later paintings show a change. In the Louvre there's a portrait of Pompadour by Quentin de La Tour. There she is in her patterned silk dress with her globe and viola, volumes of the *Encyclopédie*, architectural drafts and letters. She is the late thirties woman of education and influence, although she still shows us her pretty ankle. Also in the Louvre is a wonderful sculpture by Pigalle: *Madame de Pompadour en amitié*. It portrays La Pompadour as a mythic virgin – a muse perhaps, or a temple priestess. It announces her changed but still privileged relationship with the King – from mistress of his heart, to companion, guide and trusted confidante. She created her own image, and periodically reshaped and updated it. In modern parlance, she re-branded herself. And see, as the rue du Faubourg Saint-Honoré turns into rue Saint-Honoré, here's Gucci and Hermès and Dior – all busy updating their images to strengthen the value of their brands.

Now I come across one of the most fashionable new shops in Paris, Colette, at number 213 rue Saint-Honoré. This is a modern style emporium that specializes, as they say in Colette-speak, in 'styledesignartfood'. This shop is about beautiful things, and the aspirations of the people who buy them. It's all light, fresh and bright here. I stroll downstairs, mistakenly finding myself in a stainless steel underground café. Too shy to leave, I sit and order a café crème which I don't drink. I don't like this place much; there are dozens rather like it in Sydney. And anyway, I always prefer old fashionable places to new ones.

But the visit is worth it: a modern Brigitte Bardot enchants all the waiters as she lingers over a cigarette, her thick honey hair tumbling, long legs encased in tight jeans, complete with a tiny pink knitted sweater and pink kitten-heeled mules. I am captivated too, by her skin and eyes, by her sheen and gloss. She exerts absolute dominance over the room. Funnily enough, it doesn't seem to diminish my femininity; somehow it enhances it. She is the overt manifestation of a force all women share.

And then I cut back, take a right off rue Saint-Honoré and slip into the flattering shadows of teashop Ladurée at 16 rue Royale. This is more like it. I sigh with pleasure as I take a cup of tea and a macaroon alongside a couple of immaculate old French ladies and their toothless dogs in a pretty, painted room. For a while I sit peacefully, staring into space, thinking of the beautiful scarf I just saw, and wondering if I can ever justify paying so much for a small square of silk. Suddenly I realize that, in my happy daze, preoccupied with the beauty of the street and the shop windows, I've walked straight past two of the buildings I most wanted to see.

Number 41 rue du Faubourg Saint-Honoré is the American Ambassador's residence. Lots of worthy diplomats have no doubt lived there, but only one of them interests me: Ambassador Pamela Digby Churchill Hayward Harriman, who reigned from May 1993 to her death in 1997. Pamela Harriman lived by a simple equation: she would give pleasure to men; they would reward her in return. An English nobleman's daughter, she married Randolph Churchill, Winston's only son, and spent World War Two learning about politics and power at Winston's knee. During that time she had an affair with American President Roosevelt's personal envoy, Averell Harriman. After the war, her marriage over, she drifted to Paris where she became, of all things, a twentieth-century courtesan. Her lovers included Aly Khan, Stavros Niar-

chos, Elie de Rothschild and Gianni Agnelli. Eventually
she found another husband, the American theater pro-
ducer Leland Hayward, and when he died she reunited
with her old flame, Averell Harriman. He died leaving her
immensely wealthy.

Pamela was a chameleon: she reconfigured herself to be
whatever her lovers wanted her to be. Gianni Agnelli
wanted her to be sexy and elegant: she dressed head to toe
in couture. Her mirroring was so assiduous that old
friends giggled when Pamela answered her phone with a
phoney Italian accent. *Prrrrronto?* she'd say. Elie de Rothschild liked a woman who was quiet in bed and lovely to
wake up to, a woman of elegance and refinement: Pamela
rigorously educated herself in antiques and nineteenth-
century art. When Pamela married showbiz impresario
Leland Howard, amazed visitors watched as she played the
homespun partner, bringing out her husband's slippers
and gently sliding them on his feet. She travelled with
Leland for the out-of-town tryouts, packing an electric
frying pan so she could rustle up his favorite chicken hash
after the show. With Averell Harriman, she straightened
up into the model political wife – elegant, charitably
inclined, gracious.

It must take a lot of effort to make oneself so attractive
to men, a lot of self-discipline. To pander to their foibles
and weaknesses, to laugh at their jokes, to turn away from
the hurts and insults of those who always returned to their
wives. Americans always sniggered at Pamela (*the widow of
opportunity*, they chortled), the British had looked down
on her, but the French very much appreciated this throw-
back to an earlier era. They appreciated the craft, the art,
the self-discipline of the courtesan. Like all great artists,
she made the hard work look easy.

When she became a rich and influential widow, Pamela got a facelift, put on a power suit and played the role of Ambassador with the flair she applied to all her performances. Naturally, she was very much inclined to whitewash her past: she never really finished a degree at the Sorbonne. I wish I'd looked at the Embassy closely: it must have been a secret thrill for Pamela to take charge of a former Rothschild residence, a balm to the wound she endured when Elie de Rothschild refused to marry her so many years before.

Once, when working in Paris as an Australian diplomat, my friend Ellen turned up at the American Embassy for a Christmas party. As she came through the security entrance, she saw the guards vetting a huge box filled with assorted perfumes and champagne: a Christmas tribute to Ambassador Harriman from President Mitterrand. At the end of her life, finally, it was Pamela's turn to be courted and wooed.

The other house I walked straight past was 39 rue du Faubourg Saint-Honoré, the former Hôtel de Charost, now the British Embassy. This house belonged to Napoleon's favorite sister, Pauline, who bought it in 1803. Metternich, later Austrian Chancellor, said of Pauline that she was *as pretty as it is possible to be. She was in love with herself, and her only occupation was pleasure.* For Pauline, pleasure consisted in her worshipping her own image. She once commissioned a life-size nude sculpture of herself in white marble: her mortified husband immediately hustled Canova's masterpiece out of France to a basement in Italy. Pauline's narcissism had a familial flavor; she adored her brother Napoleon, whose glories added shine to her beauty. When the tide turned against Napoleon, Pauline's vanity became a virtue. She selflessly accompanied Napoleon on his first exile to Elba; she sold her jewels and houses to support him after his downfall; and she was still trying to improve living conditions for him when he died on St Helena. All her life, her *only occupation was pleasure*, and yet, at the last, she took pleasure in actions that were entirely admirable.

As I sit in the teashop with the old ladies, I think about La Pompadour and Pamela Harriman and Pauline Bonaparte. And I ponder on pleasure and the price we pay to give it – or to get it. Nancy Mitford saw pleasure as a kind of moral good. In her letters, thousands of them, she never dwelled on her times of loneliness or ill-health: in her view, such self-indulgence would only diminish the pleasure of the receiver. A woman's allure, and her effort to retain that appeal, was also part of her necessary social contribution. Nancy Mitford appreciated La Pompadour for the pleasure she gave to others and for the incomparable legacy of beauty she left behind.

Nancy Mitford was close friends with successors to Pauline Bonaparte in the Hôtel de Charost, British Ambassador Duff Cooper and his wife, Diana Cooper. Aristocratic and eccentric, the couple created a golden post–World War Two era. Their parties were legendary: they imported a thousand red roses for one *fête* alone. Cecil Beaton, Jean Cocteau and Noel Coward were regular guests – as well, of course, as Nancy Mitford. Diana once organized a 'Charles Ritchie Week' for a junior Canadian Embassy official who had complained that nobody ever paid any attention to him, despite the very important things he had to say. At his every arrival a band played a tune specially composed for him. Nancy Mitford painted five hundred balloons with the slogan 'Remember Ritchie!' which were released from the Embassy courtyard with postcards attached asking the recipients to send them to Ritchie with their good wishes. Several came back from Eastern Europe; one from Norway.

Duff and Diana were devoted to each other, so much so that they never denied each other their separate pleasures. At one stage Duff's lover, French writer Louise de Valmorin (on whom Nancy Mitford based the character of Albertine, Charles-Edouard's 'intoxicating old mistress' in *The Blessing*), moved into the Embassy with the couple. Diana remonstrated vigorously with her husband when he cheated on Louise. The great beauty of her day, Diana accepted lavish gifts from besotted millionaires: the *coat of shame* she blithely called her mink, gift of an admiring industrialist. Whenever Diana and Duff were apart they wrote magical daily love letters, and Diana was devastated when Duff died.

Diana and Duff's life together was characterized by their uninhibited pursuit of pleasure. But they lived in a serious age, and their brand of high frivolity was considered faintly immoral. Today we face an altogether different problem. We live in an era that glorifies self-gratification and we are constantly exhorted – instructed – to do whatever we want. *Just do it!* shouts the slogan. What's more, we are bombarded with advertising images that purport to know exactly what it is that we want, what will give us pleasure. *This* car, *this* dress, *that* lifestyle.

But an age of self-gratification is not, it seems to me, the same thing as an age of pleasure. Amid the welter of choices, sometimes it's hard to detect and honor that which genuinely gives us delight. I suspect that one of the secrets to happiness lies in making this distinction.

Edith Wharton has a wonderful description of the kind of pleasure the city of Paris can give:

Her senses luxuriated in all its material details: the thronging motors, the brilliant shops, the novelty and daring of the women's dresses, the piled-up colours of the ambulant flower-carts, the appetizing expanse of the fruiterers' windows, even the chromatic effects of the petits fours behind the plate-glass of the pastry-cooks: all the surface-sparkle and variety of the inexhaustible streets of Paris.

This description sums up for me the complexity and sophistication of the delights of Paris. And it takes us back to La Pompadour, a woman who knew that the art of giving and receiving pleasure lies in careful attention to detail.

When Pompadour died on a cold January day in 1764, her body was carried on the road out of Versailles. The King stood on his balcony and cried for his lovely friend.

As I head back to the Marais, I recall President de Gaulle's complaint about living in Pompadour's former home. *Really*, he said, *I should have set myself up at the Louvre – the 8th arrondissement is not a place for making History.*

But then, of course, he was a man.

⚜

Later, lying on my white bed at Rachel's house, I reflect on the intensely felt pleasures of a day in Paris. You know, I don't have some misguided fantasy that I would like to live here. First, foremost and forever I am an Australian citizen. Australia is my patch of the world. It's where I belong, where I am, at least in part, responsible for what happens. But here in Paris I know I can let down my guard, because what happens here is not, even in part, my responsibility. Here, I take a holiday from citizenship.

Americans have always honored Paris: they appreciate it as a bulwark against ugly modernity, it's the anti-America, the place where beauty and reason resist the sterile blandishments of Hollywood and therapy and plastic surgery and consumerism and talk-show emotions. (Oscar Wilde, *The Picture of Dorian Gray*: *'They say that when good Americans die they go to Paris,' chuckled Sir Thomas. 'Really! And where do bad Americans go when they die?' inquired the Duchess. 'They go to America,' murmured Lord Henry.*)

Australians don't, on the whole, cherish Paris. When an Australian tells you you're a Francophile, it's generally less an observation, more an accusation. Just the term itself is loaded.

Here's how, in certain Sydney circles, a Francophile might be defined: *a lightweight who buys sentimental books about house renovating in Provence and pays too much for French crockery.*

In Canberra foreign policy circles, a Francophile: *a lightweight out of step with Australia's strategic destiny in Asia.*

On the left, a Francophile: *a lightweight who negligently ignores the evil history of French nuclear testing in the South Pacific.*

On the right, a Francophile: *a traitor who ignores France's disgraceful refusal to open its markets to Australian agricultural products.*

Pointless to say: but I don't love France, I only love Paris. This only increases the crime, suggesting an atrocious refinement of decadence (*oooh, so we only love PARIS, do we?*).

Some Australians can get away with their embarrassing little secret by affecting a witty postmodern ironic affection for Paris. But I can't. I feel shamelessly pleased by Paris, captivated by it.

Paris makes me feel better.

7

Salons

*. . . so equally minute is the care required, in preparing
a soufflé or a salon.*

Edith Wharton

ONE OF MY FAVORITE rituals is to browse through the
books and magazines at the WH Smith bookstore on rue
de Rivoli, and then take afternoon tea at Angelina's nearby
salon de thé.

This afternoon the main salon is full, as usual, of tourists
and old ladies and couples and refined Englishwomen in
pale trench-coats and neat Frenchwomen with their
mothers-in-law. The room is big and high-ceilinged, yet
painted, pretty and intimate. I set myself up with a fragrant
cup of tea in one hand and a crisp new book in the other
as the hum of conversation weaves a light blanket of sound.

I always fancied the idea of hosting a salon, or even just

attending one: of being part of a salon set. Just the word
hints at a life both elegant and intellectual, which is
possibly my ideal combination. I used to think inadequate
funds or social status were the main barriers to my career
as salonnière (and yes, starting out adult life in a reeking
university shared house in Surry Hills didn't help). But a
minimal amount of reading soon revealed that even the
most privileged have found salon-making hard work. *So
minute is the care required*, as the meticulous Edith Wharton
said. Sheer social determination was never enough; magic
was also required, an alchemy, to bring the right people to
the right place at the right time and spark them to genius.

Of course, on paper a salon is simply a small society of
people who meet ritually for conversation. The first salonnière was Madame de Rambouillet, who constructed her
charming home at the beginning of the seventeenth
century for that very purpose. It was located on the site of
the present-day antique center, le Louvre des Antiquaires,
just a bit further along from here, down rue de Rivoli,
opposite the Louvre.

But in practice a great salon is a rare thing, and, while
people still talk about 'salons' in New York and London, in
truth the salon as high art seems to have died out altogether.

The most important principle governing the salon was
that it was the political and social domain of older women.
Their influence lay in the force of their individual personalities, not by weight of numbers. Edith Wharton, who
had access to some of the last nineteenth-century French
salons, thought the ideal ratio was five subtle and sophisticated women to every twenty men. Voltaire talked
appreciatively of salons *presided over by a woman who in her
declining beauty shines by her awakening wit.*

And perhaps because older women are more sensitive

to the effects of lighting, salons were sunset rituals, the conversation framed by candles and flickering fire and pale moon rays through slender windows. Nancy Mitford imagined the eager Frenchman *ready to sit up all night with some brilliant and sympathetic hostess . . .*

For Edith Wharton, an indispensable feature of salon style was what she called 'general' conversation: conversation as collaborative performance. *Raconteur* is a French word but an English concept, and nothing deadens conversation faster than the bluff fellow with his long yarns and deferred punchlines. Worse still is the confessional type. At one dinner Mrs Wharton was mortified to find herself engaged by a fellow American in the monopolizing style so beloved by her countrymen. She squirmed with boredom and embarrassment: he had no idea how crude his one-on-one style seemed to his French hosts. Nancy Mitford explained that, if the salon hostess personally accompanied you to the front door, this was a silent but unmistakeable sign that you were *not welcome again.*

By contrast, a good salon guest carefully calibrated his or her social value: the least witty should always give airtime to the most witty. Many hostesses had their great man – a writer or artist, usually – who at least nominally formed the center of the coterie and to whom the other guests deferred. Writer Félicité de Genlis, a salonnière during the heyday of salons in the eighteenth century, used to say that *if you wanted to succeed in the world, it was necessary, when entering a salon, that your vanity should bow to that of others.*

One common misapprehension is that the provision of good food and drink will guarantee a display of wit and repartee. I can offer a number of my own dinner parties as clear evidence that this is a fallacy. *She tried to found a salon, and only succeeded in opening a restaurant,* wrote Oscar Wilde, pinpointing the grave social risk involved. In fact, some of the most famous Parisian salonnières were remarkably skimpy in their offerings. In the eighteenth century, Madame Geoffrin served omelette. In the nineteenth, Princesse Mathilde provided such dreadful food that her assembly of writers used to finish up their meals in the creepy grandeur of rue de Courcelles and then hotfoot it round to the Champs-Élysées house of La Païva, a courtesan who served high-quality food in a low, glitzy atmosphere. The famous Saturday evenings *chez* Miss Stein and Miss Toklas were also abstemious. Alice was a great cook, but she only served puritan tea to the great artists and their long-suffering wives.

For Edith Wharton the salon represented the very best of France in all its urbanity, gaiety and intellect. Above all, it represented the triumph of the intellectual woman.

> *The famous French 'Salon', the best school of talk and of ideas that the modern world has known, was based on the belief that the most stimulating conversation in the world is between intelligent men and women who see each other often enough to be on terms of rank and easy friendship. Think what an asset to the mental life of any country such a group of women forms! And in France, they were not then, and they are not now, limited to the small class of the wealthy and fashionable. In France, as soon as a woman has a personality, social circumstances permit her to make it felt.*

I very much doubt if Edith Wharton is right when she says that access to salons was not limited to a small class: by their nature they were elite. But it was true that money and status weren't enough: to make the grade in the salon you had to contribute something special to the discourse.

I gave up early on a career as salonnière, but it seems to me now that I have spent a lot of time trying to find an analogue. The search for the best conversations led me down some curious paths. The Australian Broadcasting Corporation was one. As a university student I was a part-time research assistant in the rural department and later, briefly, worked on an international current affairs program. I imagined men and women of noble intent, carefully distilling truth and disinterestedly conveying it to the nation. And I did meet some men and women like that, but mostly I found a lot of tired male sexists with seventies' hairdos who were still banging on about their pet causes. The modern world seemed a faraway place in the laminated corridors of Gore Hill.

I was accepted into the Foreign Affairs Department in 1987. This was quite something, a sign that I was on a career path at last. On our first day in the great old building in Canberra, one of our lecturers was a former High Commissioner to Fiji. He was still wearing his pale green safari suit with a shark's tooth around his neck. I was shaken but not deterred. The next day our training course topics included *Diplomatic dinners: how to make people feel at home who you wish were at home* and *What to do when Australians send their mad relatives to YOUR post*. Mmm. Eventually, of course, I did get to eavesdrop on serious conversations, but not nearly as often as I had expected.

Things got a lot better when I joined the Prime Minister's Department, and worked in the international affairs area. This was the real deal. I wrote briefing notes for the Prime Minister, I attended his meetings, I tiptoed the corridors of power. I got to listen in on a really high class of conversation. The first Gulf War happened during my time in the Prime Minister's Department, and the Dili massacre in East Timor. Serious matters were at hand, the national interest was at stake, I played my own small role.

I would like to say that working for the Deputy Prime Minister was the most intellectually fascinating time of my life. It *was* amazing in many ways. But as a rule, stimulating and equal conversation between men and women is not a Labor Party strong point, *maaaaate*.

And as for the management consultants . . . but that, of course, is why I am here.

The philosopher David Hume, one of those enlightened Scots who found France so delightful in the eighteenth century, relished the difference between the British and French approaches to women and society. An evening in England generally concluded with the ladies gracefully exiting the room, leaving the men to cigars, port and politics. In France, by contrast, men and women *mixed* in all circumstances of life. Women were considered indispensable to the creation of fine society. Women and men were equally expected to step up to the conversational mark – to be familiar with the great ideas, issues and arts of the age – and to be able to discuss them with wit and intelligence.

David Hume knew a lot about French women because he was lucky enough to attend the greatest salon of all. In some respects Madame du Deffand seems an unlikely candidate for salonnière. Separated from her provincial husband, modest in title and means, she lived most of her life on the generosity of others. At fifty she went blind. Yet, through the force of her intellect and personality, she rose to become the greatest salonnière in history.

Night after night, year after year, from 1746 until her death in 1780, in colored silks, satin shoes and matching stockings, with their powdered hair and beauty patches, aristocrats and scientists, authors and diplomats, foreign visitors and local wits came gratefully to Madame du Deffand's dramatic gold and crimson salon. Perched on pretty chairs, they flirted, joked, played cards or discussed the latest books. Benjamin Franklin came by, as did Horace Walpole and yes, the delighted Scot, David Hume. One of the assembly might read aloud a letter from one of Madame du Deffand's many correspondents: the French ambassador in Constantinople sending tales of Turkish splendor; her good friend Madame de Choiseul with insider gossip from the court at Versailles; best of all, the great Voltaire himself, firing philosophical bombshells and political *bons mots* from the safety of his estate in Switzerland.

Framed like a statue in her winged chair, the sovereign of this tiny kingdom of pleasure was Madame du Deffand herself. Having slept all day, she was ready to sit up all night. As her guests arrived, Madame du Deffand's blank eyes would turn towards them and her knowing fingers would roam in light greeting over their faces, as if to dissect the personality within. And her guests needed their composure, for Madame du Deffand's salon was no place for the socially feeble. This was the peak of the eighteenth century, the age of wit and ridicule, brilliance and *bel esprit*, and most of all, reason. Not earnest, cardigan-wearing, look-at-all-sides-of-the-question kind of reason, but sparkling, kitten-heeled, stay-up-all-night and fuck-you kind of reason. Madame du Deffand's restless hands once paused lightly on the heart of the reserved man of letters, Monsieur Fontenelle. *There too, lies a brain*, she said, approvingly.

Madame du Deffand was a martinet about gaiety. She banned the serious, the didactic, the *improving*. And in this she rendered herself a conservative, for the world around her was changing. As the gay and refined Age of Reason headed towards its revolutionary climax, Madame du Deffand clung to the old codes. She and her friends scoffed at the encyclopedists' faith in progress; they derided the new vogue for sentimentality. They wore their licentiousness and cynicism with ancient pride.

A night at Madame du Deffand's was a festival of one-liners.

When Monsieur de Plessis-Chatillon lamented his first wife's death to his second wife, she replied, quick as a flash: *'Let me assure you, Monsieur, no one regrets that tragedy more than I.'*

When an ageing admirer humbly admitted to the Duchesse de la Vallière that he had long loved her without having the courage to declare himself, the equally decrepit libertine laughed out loud. *'My God, why did you not tell me?'* she mocked. *'You could have had me like all the others.'*

Madame du Deffand was the hardest and funniest of them all. Once she was invited to supper at the home of Madame de Marchais. Madame du Deffand replied that she would need to spend time with her lover of nearly fifty years, Monsieur de Pont de Veyle, who was very ill. She agreed, however, to try to stop by for a moment before going to her friend's sickbed. Madame du Deffand arrived promptly for the party at nine o'clock. To everyone's surprise, she announced gaily: *'I've come to have supper with you all.'* Of course, the assembly asked for news of her lover. *'Oh,'* said Madame du Deffand, airily, *'he died. If he hadn't, I wouldn't be here.'*

These anecdotes are all well-documented, for Madame du Deffand's gatherings and guests regularly featured in a select newsletter sent to Enlightened monarchs around

Europe, including Frederick of Prussia, Catherine the Great in Russia and Gustav III in Sweden, all of whom hungered for news of Paris, the capital of the world. Imagine the grateful guest storing mental notes and arriving home to record the *bons mots* in the pale light of dawn.

One of the great pleasures of salon life lay in promoting your friends and feuding with your enemies. Madame du Deffand and Voltaire shared a particular loathing for the fashionable philosopher Jean-Jacques Rousseau. Rousseau claimed that man was better off in a state of nature than in sinful human society. Madame du Deffand hated this concept: her entire life had been devoted to getting as far away from nature as possible. Voltaire was outraged by the idea, which he saw as turning back the clock on human progress.

On receiving Rousseau's *Discourse on Inequality* in 1755, Voltaire wrote to the author.

I have received your book against the human race. I thank you for it. No one has ever employed so much intellect in the attempt to prove us beasts. A desire seizes us to walk on all four paws when we read your work. Nevertheless, as it is more than sixty years since I lost the habit, I feel, unfortunately, that it is impossible for me to resume it.

There was another thing about Rousseau. He, along with other important intellectuals like Diderot, was promoting an essentially bourgeois ideal of women's behavior. These philosophers wanted women to be stoic mothers, moral guides and patient, silent, faithful supporters of their men. It was the intellectual equivalent of the artistic gulf between the frivolous aristocratic

Boucher and dour bourgeois Chardin. As vigorously as they advocated the rights and liberties of men, they simultaneously endorsed stricter limitations on women. Madame du Deffand's rigorous adherence to the aristocratic model was, in its way, a defence of the existing social order that guaranteed her own freedoms.

A few years ago, French intellectual Mona Ozouf explained this paradox, arguing that the *ancien régime* was good for women: *In a monarchical society, every man's passions are exerted in defending his privileges, holding and marking his place, which opens a wide field of action for women's savoir-faire, the sureness of their psychological sense, the fertility of their imagination . . . It is therefore not surprising that they reigned in France.*

Jean-Jacques Rousseau was well aware of the importance of Madame du Deffand, so much so that he tried to explain away their lack of social connection.

I at first began by being very interested in Madame du Deffand, the loss of whose sight made her an object of pity in mine, but her way of life, so unlike mine that one of us rose almost as the other retired, her unlimited passion for the trivialities of the 'bel esprit', the importance she attached, good or bad, to the least scribblings which appeared, the despotism and passion of her judgements, her exaggerated infatuation with things or hatred of them which caused her to speak of everything convulsively with unbelievable prejudice, her invincible stubbornness, the unreasoning enthusiasm into which she was thrown by the obstinacy of her passionate opinions; all that soon discouraged me from giving her the attention I had wished.

He concludes on a note of high vanity. *I neglected her and she noticed it. That was enough to put her into a rage and although I sense how much a woman of her character was to be feared, I preferred to expose myself to the scourge of her hatred than that of her friendship.*

No one was fooled – whatever illusions he may have comforted himself with, friendship with Madame du Deffand was never an option for the sexist, dullish Mr Rousseau.

⚜

There's the real Paris and there's another Paris, a three-dimensional model formed in my mind's eye after months of looking at maps. This Paris is compact, neat, with a twisting Seine, the spiral swirl of the *arrondissements*, the white bump of Montmartre, and the cartoon pop-ups of the Eiffel Tower and the Arc de Triomphe. Now, as I wander down the seemingly never-ending rue Saint-Dominique in the quiet Faubourg Saint-Germain, I'm reminded again that the real Paris always comes up bigger and grander than my imaginings.

The buildings on this street seem to have sprung from the soil, so harmonious is their composition. This is civilization, old and sure, calm and resigned. And quiet. If I were to so much as cough I'm sure my voice would bounce and echo crudely off the seventeenth-century buildings. I'm looking for numbers 10–12, the former Couvent des Filles de St Joseph, built in 1641.

Oh. I see now why it's so quiet around here. This whole block is the Ministry of Defence complex. I stop at a courtyard gate, in front of two soldiers with machine guns. They combine high fashion with extreme menace.

I peek past them as I say, 'Could you point out to me Madame du Deffand's apartment?'

They look at each other blankly, two distractingly handsome killers.

'Never heard of her,' says one.

Not again.

'But you must,' I protest. 'She was a famous salonnière.'

'Well,' says the other one, 'there was Madame Mère, Napoleon's mother, she lived here in the Hôtel de Brienne.'

Really? But I know he's talking about the other building in the block.

'No,' I say stubbornly, shaking my head, 'it's Madame du Deffand. She lived here. In the old convent.'

The killers smile at me. Then their faces revert to their default expression of immaculate boredom.

⚜

Madame du Deffand was the greatest salonnière of all, but that's not the real reason I am interested in her. I care about what she created, but even more, I care about what she overcame.

Brace yourself, for this is the voice of utter despair: *For myself, Monsieur,* writes Madame du Deffand to Voltaire, *I admit that I have only one fixed idea, one feeling, one sorrow, one misfortune, it is the pain of having been born; there is no part to be played on the world's theater to which I do not prefer nothingness, and, what will appear to be of no consequence to you, is that when I have the final proof of having to return to it, my horror of death will be none the less.*

This is the real Madame du Deffand, whose salon was the gayest in Paris, but whose voice is as modern, as sterile and as empty as the twentieth century. All conditions were the same to her, *from the angel to the oyster.* The great, overriding misfortune was to have been born at all.

Madame du Deffand spent her whole life trying to

manage the intolerable burden of existence. She found
comfort nowhere. Even as a child she saw through the
idea of God. Anyway, the Bible lacked taste. Nature she
never cared for, and the boredom of country life was
insupportable. Relationships? As far as she could tell, the
ties that bound people together were more about habit or
mutual need than sincere, disinterested affection. Married
off to a rural Marquis, Madame du Deffand found nothing
in him or family relationships to give value to her life.
When her sister, who came specifically to Paris to live near
her and look after her, died, Madame du Deffand merely
commented: *She was a good woman, but for whom one could
have no feeling.* She never wanted a child: Madame du
Deffand was glad she had not condemned another person
to the torment of life's long blank meaninglessness.

Even the tragedy of her blindness did not distract
Madame du Deffand from her misery; as she maintained
to Voltaire:

> *You do not know and you cannot know from personal experience,
> the condition of those who think, who reflect, who have some
> activity, and who are at the same time without talent, without
> passion, without occupation, without diversion; who have had
> friends but who have lost them without being able to replace them;
> add to that a delicacy of taste, a little discernment, a great love of
> truth; put out those people's eyes, and place them in the middle
> of Paris, of Peking, in fact of anywhere you like and I maintain
> that it would be happier for them not to have been born . . . all
> physical ills, however great (except for pain), sadden and depress
> the soul less than human converse and society.*

What do you do if you are an eighteenth-century aristocrat for whom life is utterly meaningless? In 1718 you go

straight to Paris, of course, on your way to hell. When
Madame du Deffand arrived in the capital at the age of
twenty-two she turned to *continuous excessive dissipation*.
She gambled and drank too much and slept around. She
used people. She wearily scaled the social heights: she even
had a brief affair with the Regent of France and extracted
a lifelong pension from him. Nothing satisfied, of course,
and in the end she was bored, bored, bored. Not only this,
but at thirty-two, after the death of the Regent, she became
a social outcast. They said of her that she was a *laughing
stock, blamed by everyone, despised by her lover, abandoned by her
friends; she no longer knows how to untangle it all*. But no one
despised Madame du Deffand more than she despised
herself: *I am left to myself, and I cannot be in worse hands*, she
said. *I search for my soul and I find only the remainder of it*.

In Lawrence Durrell's *The Alexandria Quartet*, a character observes that each of us lives by *selective fictions*.
I think he meant that, perhaps unconsciously, each
of us devises a narrative to impose some structure and
meaning on our random, chaotic lives. But Madame du
Deffand denied herself the consolations of grand expla-
nations like religion or fate or genetics. She equally
refused to indulge herself in the little lies that make life
bearable. Instead she lived her life bravely in the cold,
bleak vacuum of doubt.

Anita Brookner, in her survey *Romanticism and its Discontents*, quotes Madame du Deffand's searching question: *Mais,
M. de Voltaire, vous combattez et détruisez toutes les erreurs, mais
que mettez-vous à leur place? Monsieur de Voltaire, you combat
and destroy all the errors, but what do you put in their place?*

Today, of course, we would rush Madame du Deffand
to pharmacologists, who would prescribe drugs for
her depression. *Chemical imbalance*, they'd say. *Childhood*

trauma. Hormones. Voltaire himself saw the deep emotional factors involved in Madame du Deffand's agony: *You give me great pain, Madame; for your sad ideas result not only from reasoning: they come from the feelings.*

Voltaire thought the answer was to encourage Madame du Deffand to use her considerable intellectual gifts. *All that is beautiful and luminous is of your element,* he wrote to her in 1736. *Do not be afraid of discussion. Do not be ashamed to add the strength of your intelligence to the charms of your person. Make your ties with the other women, but speak reason to me.*

But Madame du Deffand refused to indulge in the fiction that her talents were in any way comparable to those of the great Voltaire. She wrote back:

> *Happy is he who is born with great intelligence and great talents! And how much to be pitied is he who has just enough to prevent him from vegetating. I find myself in that class and am among many. The only difference between me and my fellows is that they are pleased with themselves and that I am far from being pleased with them and even further from being pleased with myself.*

So here is Madame du Deffand, painfully alive to the moral and spiritual agony of conscious existence. And her response? Not a conventional one, that's for sure. Not suicide, nor faith, nor drink or drugs as diversions from doubt. No. She chose a most unlikely path for survival. She chose society, gaiety, *reason.*

Deffand took the salon code as a kind of regime. She chose logic over instinct, reason over feeling, art over nature. With an unwavering commitment she upheld an aristocratic code of living based on careless erudition, classical impartiality and casual wit. Society became her salve, if not her salvation.

It gave her a reason to get up in the evening.

And it worked. In the candle-lit glitter of her gold and crimson salon she created a whole world. Even when she was seventy years old, the English aesthete Horace Walpole thought she was *an old blind debauchée of wit*. She was *very old and stone blind*, Walpole acknowledged, *but retains all vivacity, wit, memory, judgement, passions and agreeableness. She corresponds with Voltaire, dictates charming letters to him, con- tradicts him, is no bigot to him or anybody, laughs both at the clergy and the philosophers.*

But it must be said: Madame du Deffand was not a nice woman. She was never happy or kind. Even her friends were frightened of her, and her lovers treated her with wary caution as though she were a particularly dangerous prized pet. Her enemies were delighted when she devel- oped an unlikely and unrequited passion for the younger, homosexual Walpole – at last she exhibited the needs of an ordinary woman.

Madame du Deffand took a *protégée* once, her lovely niece Julie de Lespinasse, and then expelled her when the young woman attracted her own circle of admirers. In 1764, Julie's supporters gave her a house, literally on the next corner from Madame du Deffand in rue de Bellechasse.

As I wander back down the street I can see a few Defence bureaucrats lounging on the grass in the sunshine: this little park is all that remains of Julie's place. There must have been extraordinary human traffic here on moonlit nights as guests left Madame du Deffand's to sneak off to Julie's rival salon down the road. Julie died romantically young at age forty-four in 1776, mourned by all except the woman who intro- duced her to Paris. Madame du Deffand merely observed: *Mademoiselle de Lespinasse died this night, two hours after midnight; it would have meant something to me once, today it is nothing at all.*

Madame du Deffand died at home in 1780 at the age of eighty-four, surrounded by people, as always. On her deathbed she consented to receive the priest, but it was said that she couldn't resist lecturing him on the proper style: *Father, you will be very pleased with me; but grant me three favours: no questions, no reasons, no sermons.*

⚜

Back down the road, I make my way to a modest family restaurant with lace curtains. Monsieur welcomes me with cool formality. There's no phoney assumption of familiarity. No cheesy questions. Even the facial expressions are sober, discreet. Paradoxically, perhaps, this creates a space in which I have my personal privacy and my comfort. It's why being a woman alone for lunch feels perfectly comfortable.

As I sit down to look at the menu it occurs to me that many people would not admire Madame du Deffand for choosing 'society' as a way of life, as a meaning for life. To many this would seem unbearably shallow.

Partly the modern disdain for social forms arises because we are, all of us, Romantics. It's not a matter of choice: this is the point of history in which we find ourselves. Ever since Rousseau idealized the noble savage and Beethoven refused to bow his head to a nobleman and Byron tossed his raven curls, good manners, forms, etiquette, courtesies, all these have been devalued. The individual has been encouraged to raise his or her feelings above the interests of the social group. Moreover, in the Romantic world view, civic society itself is downgraded – in the cities the individual finds only the stale rituals of a worn-out world.

In nature alone can man find genuine honesty and grand sensations.

But agreed forms of social discourse are not foolish things. They are necessary to civilization. In the course of the French Revolution, as French society was trying to recover from the end of the monarchy and the Terror and to find some way to reconstruct itself as a Republic, politician and novelist Germaine de Staël offered this caution against barbarousness, against wilfully abandoning all the old courtesies:

> *Civilized manners, like the good taste they are part of, have great literary and political importance . . . Politeness is the bond established by society between men who are strangers to one another. Virtues attach us to family, friends and people less fortunate than ourselves; but in every relationship which we do not characterise as a duty, civilized manners prepare the way for affections, make belief easier, and preserve for each man the position his merit should give him in the world . . .*

Her comments weren't about some frivolous objective of social ease in the new Republic. At that perilous period of transition, Germaine de Staël recognized that a society's manners were an indicator of the health of the entire body politic. *Social conventions are the image of moral life,* she wrote, *presupposing it in any circumstances which do not give a chance of proving it: they keep men in the habit of respecting each other's options. If a state's leaders damage or despise these conventions, they themselves will no longer be able to inspire this respect, the elements of which they themselves have destroyed.*

Now, at the extreme historical end of Romanticism, we only have to watch reality television at night to recognize that today even reason is regarded with suspicion, morally overthrown in favor of fleeting emotions and basic instincts. Sense has been dumped for sensibility.

Henry James and Edith Wharton were fascinated by these themes. Each of them contrasted American 'naturalness' with European sophistication and worldliness. The curious thing is that, in their literature, both Henry James and Edith Wharton tended to deliver their verdict in favor of American innocence: my favorite Jamesian heroine is Isabel Archer, an American innocent most cruelly duped by corrupted Continental (or continentalized) sophisticates. But in life, good for them, Henry and Edith ran from barbarous America. They chose Europe and civilization; they chose sophisticated, worldly, *mannered* societies.

The Romantics forgot one thing: the city is vital because it is where *civilization* occurs. Critics talk about cities being cold, abstract, anonymous places. But it's a matter of judgement whether this is a prelude to vice or a blessed advantage. My mother couldn't wait to leave her poking and prying country town for the freedom of the city. She was suffocating in the wide open spaces: only on the crowded sidewalk could she breathe. Madame du Deffand felt the same. She was often unhappy in Paris but that wasn't the point. Only in Paris could she exercise her formidable powers – could she be herself, or more specifically, could she create herself. For Madame du Deffand, Paris meant society and civilization and personal freedom. *You need Paris*, said Voltaire helpfully to his friend.

The single advantage of the country, as far as Madame du Deffand was concerned, was that there you expected to be miserable: *In the provinces it is duller, but in Paris it is more unbearable. Here* [the provinces] *one expects nothing, one*

has no pretensions, no desires and one is consequently without
disgust or disappointment.

I myself have nothing against nature. In its place. I agree
that it's important, not least for humanity's own survival,
and we should look after it. Aesthetically I take the
eighteenth-century view: there's nothing wrong with a
broad and wild vista that a whole lot of pruning, culling
and an exquisite little temple pavilion couldn't rectify. I
like cut flowers and good coffee and *Vanity Fair* magazine
and Mozart and Duke Ellington and long, elegant shoes.
I don't care for pets or camping. And I hope I shall not be
maligned for this. Frankly, I think it's good news for the
wilderness if some of us don't feel an urgent need to be in
it and stomp all over it.

I think cities are where the best things happen. The city,
manners, forms, society, the community – that's the
trajectory I draw. You won't get the civic virtues anywhere else. You won't get the lurches towards freedom
anywhere else.

I once read somewhere that etiquette is an extension of
ethics. I believe this to be true. Manners impose a super-
ficial conformity, but more importantly, they provide a
framework within which we can all do pretty much what
we want. Become who we want to be. Like Madame du
Deffand, who used a framework of manners and society
to lead a life of utmost personal and intellectual freedom.

Like me, in this city, in this little restaurant, alone and at
peace, embraced by the distant courtesies.

∾ 8 ∾

The Left Bank

Young women who write seldom have much sense of
moderation (neither have old women, for that matter).

Colette

I was one of those children who could always be found in
the fork of a tree with a book. Books were insurance for
me, a way of protecting myself against unpleasant realities.
A dog-eared favorite would be discreetly propped up on
my lap at meal times; my head rising for a bite of lamb chop
and mashed potato and turning down again for another
chapter. Novels came with me in the car to Mass on
Sundays, to family reunions, to beach-side picnics. As
family and friends set up post-lunch cricket, I'd retreat
quietly to the car. 'It's so stuffy in there!' my mother would
protest, but I was cooling myself in the fresher airs of fiction.

Reading I loved, but re-reading offered the deeper
pleasure. By the time I was fourteen, and still almost

unnaturally innocent of life matters, my literary heroines were also soul mates. Isabel Archer, Dorothea Brooke, Lily Bart, Elizabeth Bennett, these were my ardent and misguided friends whose quest for a first-class life – a life of art, beauty, knowledge and true love – led them into peril. I would sob and toss at the punishments meted out to them for their high aspirations. And I, the bookish daughter of a Sydney suburban butcher, would carefully draw the lessons, cautioning herself never to be led astray by a sly American fortune hunter in Northern Italy or a reclusive pedant in provincial England or the dangerous glitter of New York society.

At school, however, the nuns had a powerful narrative of their own. Theirs was the story of the priceless value of virginity, and what a woman should be ready to do to defend it. Sister Paula would lovingly recite the gory details surrounding the murder of Saint Maria Goretti, a young virgin who told her potential rapist to go ahead and stab her to death rather than compel her to the sin of unmarried sexual intercourse. 'And yet, she forgave him on her deathbed,' she'd conclude reverently.

I grew to loathe Maria Goretti and all she represented. *Why didn't she choose to live?* I wondered. *Why didn't she submit? (It was only sex after all, and how bad can it be?) Why didn't she save her life instead of giving in to death?* Martyrs no longer appealed to me, nor angels, nor victims. I wanted women who had the courage to live, not die.

So then I shed not my innocence, for I remained woefully inexperienced, but my willingness to remain so. I wanted to banish the burden of innocence; I didn't like my perilous virgin vulnerability. Of course, in those days my answer to this need wasn't to go in search of worldly experience: I merely changed my reading habits. And I gradually uncovered a new breed of literary women – women who weren't tossed around by life, but grabbed it by the scruff of the neck and shook it hard. Heroines like Albertine in Nancy Mitford's *The Blessing*, or Colette's knowing courtesans in *Gigi* and *Chéri*, or even Anita Loos's gold-digger Lorelei Lee of *Gentlemen Prefer Blondes*, represented a new kind of femininity to me. These were vivid, wilful, forceful creatures. They wore their worldliness as a badge of honor. I still loved Dorothea Brooke and Isabel Archer, of course, but I grew rather impatient with their moral ditherings. My role models became the women who survived and prospered.

Now I pause on the river bank in my dark coat and bright lipstick and breathe the moist chilled air rising from the green Seine. The breeze rustles the dark leafy trees and cools the stones of the buildings. It lifts the coat-tails of walkers as they cross the Pont des Arts to the Left Bank.

The Left Bank, the *quartier Latin*, makes sense to me. For centuries this was the heartland of Parisian Catholicism, the home of the city's convents and monasteries, churches and spires, saints and mystics. In the nineteenth and twentieth centuries, as inexorably as experience follows innocence, the Left Bank transformed, becoming home to a new breed of Parisians – the taboo-busting artists and drug-taking bohemians, the alcoholic expatriates and the showy lesbians, the hot jazz babies and the cool intellectuals. On the Left Bank, sinfulness mingles with the sacred, and overwhelms it.

I wind down rue de Seine, stand with my back to a graffiti-covered cream wall and look across the narrow road to number 31. Above the blue courtyard door there's a little plaque. *George Sand (1804–1876)*, it announces, *lived in this house in 1831.* As I hesitate on the narrow sidewalk elegant people squeeze past me, on their way to the river perhaps, or another art gallery or antique shop. A car pulls up and blocks my view. But even in the hum of modern Paris, it's still not difficult to call up the moment when George Sand, the Baroness Aurore Dupin DuDevant, arrived in Paris.

It is a freezing January day in 1831. At twenty-seven years old Aurore Dupin has abandoned her husband, two small children and the responsibilities of her large country estate, Nohant, in the province of Berry. Impatient in her long skirts and high heels, she hurries through the blue courtyard doors to reunite with her lover, Jules Sandeau. In the nearly ten years since her marriage she has taken several lovers, but none like twenty-year-old Jules, with his angelic curls and pink and white cheeks and frail blond neediness. Later she exults to a friend: *He was there, in my own room, in my arms happy, groaning, crying, laughing, beaten, kissed, bitten. It was a storm of pleasure the like of which we have never experienced before.*

When Aurore next emerges from these courtyard doors she is unrecognizable. She and Jules look more like first-year students than lovers. She sports a long grey riding coat and tie, buttoned-up trousers and little black boots with sturdy iron heels. Her black satin eyes are still striking, but her shining black hair is pulled up under a cap. She is smoking a cigar. His cravat and vest are crooked. Together they roam the streets, attend the theater, dine at cheap restaurants and revel in down-at-the-heel, shabby, creative, bohemian Paris. They mingle with writers and artists, actors and musicians; even the great Balzac befriends them. *How dear my Paris is to me, how sweet her liberty to live in love, and to be with my Jules who loves me so*, crows Aurore.

Aurore has tasted freedom and she doesn't intend to give it up. What she now requires is an excuse to justify the permanent abandonment of the provinces. *To be an artist!* she thinks, *Yes, I want to be one*. So, just like that, she makes her plans. She will be reborn as George Sand. Her first novel, *Indiana*, about a woman's unhappy marriage and search for true love, will cause a sensation and turn her into an international celebrity. She will become a pin-up girl for Romantic singularity and wilfulness. And she will, of course, live in Paris, the capital of bohemian Romanticism.

As I stand here on rue de Seine, I am struck again by the force that was George Sand. As a young girl she was a convent student, living just a few streets away from here at rue Cardinal Lemoine. Whatever the nuns taught her, George Sand was clearly never convinced by the orthodox lessons. Her personal philosophy was alarming and sub-versive; whatever was good for her must, by definition, be good for everyone. She summed up this sublime self-centeredness: *I never asked myself why I wanted this or that*, she declared. *The inner me always proudly answered: Because I want it. That said everything*.

Thinking about George Sand and her monstrous, marvelous ego, a memory strikes me. A few months ago I became anguished as I contemplated quitting my job. There was a single moment when, all at once, a whole crowd of fears and anxieties came surging into my mind, like unwelcome partygoers. I couldn't seem to eject them, these ugly concerns about money and security and risk and ageing. Shouting noisily in my head, tossing shallow insults and dark prophecies, these interlopers drowned out all sensible conversation.

So I found a psychologist near my North Sydney office and went to sit in her room. I briefly told her my situation. 'I want to quit my job and I'm afraid,' I told her. She questioned me, drawing me out. And what's *this* telling you? she'd say. And what's *this* telling you? She talked very slowly. But it became a weirdly circular conversation.

She: 'What does this *anxiety* tell you?'

Me, cautiously: 'Well, I guess it's telling me that I am afraid . . .'

She, very slowly now: 'And what's the *fear* telling you?'

This is getting ridiculous.

Me: 'It's telling me that I'm anxious?'

I soon realized the fear was telling me that I'd rather cope with any number of emotional gatecrashers than spend another minute with this particular psychologist. At the end of our session she told me that if I were to commit to a series of discussions she was really very sure she could help me. Eventually, she implied. I thanked her, paid and quit my job the next day. And the crowd vacated my head as suddenly as it had arrived, leaving air, space and freedom. Once I'd taken charge of my fate, the world seemed a lot simpler.

George Sand never once wavered, never doubted, never reflected negatively upon her own actions. She soon grew tired of little pink and white Jules Sandeau and calmly ended their affair. But he never got over her, and he always despaired at her casual repudiation. As an old man he was heard declaring bitterly: *She is a graveyard. Do you understand? A graveyard.* A succession of lovers would pass through George Sand's life: there was Alfred de Musset, the Byronic dandy; Michel de Bourges, the married socialist lawyer; Charles Didier; Gustave de Gévaudon; the actor PF Bocage; the writer Mallefille; a disastrous one-night stand with writer Prosper Merimée; and of course, the composer Frédéric Chopin.

But no matter what turbulence she generated in her romantic life, George Sand herself was the calm in the eye of the storm. As the chaos roiled around her, she remained Buddha-like, unnaturally serene. She turned out novels as automatically as other people cook the nightly dinner. She wrote at night, starting at around midnight and finishing about 4 am before retiring. She never struggled to perfect her talents or polish her creations. Of her novel *Leone Leoni* she said: *I wrote this book in a week* [at Nohant] *and hardly read it over before sending it to Paris.* The lonely genius Flaubert once wrote to George Sand: *You don't know what it is to spend an entire day with one's head in one's hands, taxing one's poor brain in search of a word. With you, the flow of ideas is broad, continuous, like a river . . .* It was perfectly true. George replied: *I simply can't understand your anguish.*

It's a few short steps to the corner café, La Palette, where I order a beer and a plate of cheese at an outside table. It's cool all right, one of those spring days that reverts to winter, but it's good to sit here with my jacket pulled close around me and feel the bracing air against my cheeks and the sharp tang of the beer against my throat. And now, as the wind flirts with my hair, my mind steps through the years and down the street, taking a right at rue Jacob, where, on the third floor at 28, another famous French-woman made her first Parisian home. The year is 1893, fifty years after George Sand's flight to Paris. The woman is Colette, a twenty-year-old bride newly arrived from the provinces.

Unlike George Sand, the young Colette didn't find liberty in Paris. The apartment on rue Jacob was small and dark, it had *no light, no air*, it was *almost a poor man's flat* and *profoundly melancholy*. Nor did Colette find solace in the city; for this homesick country girl, Paris was an expanded prison: *I did not wish to know Paris. The town filled me with dread.*

Colette had married a wily, manipulative man fifteen years older than herself. Far from rebelling against him, she embraced her wifely servitude: *There are many scarcely nubile girls who dream of becoming the show, the plaything, the licentious masterpiece of some middle-aged man*, she said. Willy was a Parisian celebrity. He published titillating books, but a stable of writers secretly wrote them. His little country wife was in love with him, but Willy was not a good husband; he was neglectful, unfaithful and intermittent in his attentions. In the first year of her marriage Colette wilted like a plant deprived of sunshine; her illness became so grave that her mother came from the country and nursed her back to health.

When Willy told Colette to write down some of her school stories, she set about the task with agreeable indifference. She sat down in the gloomy apartment and dutifully filled the pages of her notebooks. Willy rejected her work, saying: *I was wrong. It's no use at all.* He returned to his stable of ghost-writers, to his artistic feuds and his mistresses, and Colette returned, 'relieved' to her cat, Kiki-La-Doucette, to her divan and her books, to her correspondence with her mother, to her few friends. With her long, long plait, her pointed chin and dark blue eyes, Colette was rather like a princess in a fractured fairy tale, only half-aware of her imprisonment, unconsciously waiting for her release.

It wasn't until one day five years later that Willy stumbled across the manuscript when he was cleaning out his desk. *He opened one of the copy-books, turned the pages: 'It's rather nice.' He opened a second copy-book and said no more. A third, a fourth. 'My God!' he muttered. 'I am the bloodiest fool.' He swept up the scattered copy-books just as they were, grabbed his flat-brimmed top hat and bolted to his publisher's. And that is how I became a writer,* Colette concluded, as if it were all so simple. Willy published Colette's first Claudine novel (*Claudine à l'École*) in 1900 under his own name and it was immediately a huge success.

I swallow a hard mouthful of beer with a bite of cheese and try to imagine how a born writer could spend five years of her life with her first major work tucked away in a drawer – forever, for all she knew. And then how this writer could endure a further five years in which her work was published under her husband's name. Colette's professed indifference seems remarkable: how could this woman have been so casual about her monumental gift? How could she have been so indifferent to her vocation? How could she have passively tolerated her husband's domination?

Then, by pressing Colette to write for four hours every day, Willy was rapidly able to capitalize on *Claudine*'s success with three sequels – each published under his own name.

Willy's domination lasted from his marriage to Colette in 1893 until their separation in 1906. First he persuaded his wife to accept that he would have his own mistresses. Then he encouraged Colette to pursue several lesbian relationships. Finally he pushed Colette to go on stage, laying the groundwork for her future independence. Colette, passive and unfocused, was well aware that she

wanted to separate from her husband, but in the end it was
he who delivered the final blow: . . . *what I had heard was
a dismissal. While I had been dreaming of flight, close beside
me someone had been planning to turn me quietly out of the
house – out of my own house.* She recalled the humiliation of
the marital split: *I remember the flush that crept over my cheeks,
I remember my stupidity. Deprived by fraud of something I had
wished to leave by stealth.*

Colette's journey from innocence to experience is
often portrayed as a story of calculated rebelliousness. Her
many biographers absent-mindedly refer to the occasion
when Colette left Willy – except she didn't. In the fron-
tispiece to Judith Thurman's bulky biography, *Secrets of the
Flesh*, the publisher Bloomsbury trumpets Colette as 'the
twentieth century's first modern woman'. Except she
wasn't. Perhaps these assumptions persist because the later
Colette – massive and self-assured – bore so slim a resem-
blance to the slight, timid Colette of her youth. Perhaps it
seems impossible to believe in a passive Colette, a docile
Colette. Colette re-invented herself, but she did so – at
least at first – from necessity, not choice.

Far from being modern, it seems to me that Colette was
entirely pagan. Hers was an ancient temperament. *Content
yourself, I urge you, with a passing temptation, and satisfy it,* she
told her best friend, the actress Marguerite Moreno, *What
more can one be sure of than that which one holds in one's arms,
at the moment one holds it in one's arms . . .*

When I was a little girl my parents lovingly led my little
brother and me to the end of their double bed where we
were encouraged to kneel and say our prayers before the
image of the exposed and bleeding heart of Jesus. I look
back on those occasions now with bewilderment. What is
it about Christianity and its obsession with sacrifice and

death? No doubt that's one reason why I cherish Colette's writings. She turned away from death. It didn't interest her, she always said – not even her own. When her mother died, she refused to go to her funeral or to wear mourning. As for the meaning of life, Colette simply asked: *Does one really have time to discover or create one?*

When Colette was about thirty-three an idea occurred to her. *I had become vaguely aware of a duty towards myself, which was to write something other than the Claudines.* It was at this point, I think, that Colette began her process of self-invention, less in the conscious manner of George Sand, and more like the lovely organic unfolding of a flower.

Colette simply opened up to her own gifts. As she blossomed, she naturally drew upon the prosaic clutter, the here-and-nowness of the world around her: household pets and tangled gardens, the St Tropez seaside and the Palais Royal courtyard, messy desks and stale theatrical dressing rooms, her lover's looks and her mother's advice. No experience in her life was beneath inclusion in Colette's art. And because Colette's life took some extraordinary directions, naturally she wrote about some shocking matters. On more than one occasion a newspaper began serializing one of her works (*The Pure and The Impure, The Ripening Seed*) only to stop abruptly as it became apparent just how sexually exact and explicit Colette could be. It was as if Colette actively, warmly embraced the world, the flesh, the devil.

With the air whipping up more strongly around my face, I rise and pay my bill. I stroll down to 20 rue Jacob. In 1907 American heiress Natalie Barney, a beautiful and promiscuous lesbian, bought this house. She hosted parties for literary Paris, at the end of which the female guests would celebrate their femininity by donning diaphanous

gowns and dancing in the garden temple, followed by a
cup of tea. Colette performed naked for the assembled
women on several occasions. A frustrated literary figure
reportedly once pulled out his penis and waved it at
the dancing women, shouting, *Have you never seen one of
these?*

Colette and Natalie Barney had a brief affair, and a long
friendship. Even when they were old ladies Natalie would
climb the steps of the Palais Royal to visit Colette for a
long gossip: two old dames remembering their glory days.

Standing on this gorgeous street, my heart surges as I
imagine these extraordinary and gifted women making
their way in this little corner of Paris. And even though
George Sand died just three years after Colette was born,
there's a curious link between them. It's one of those only-
in-Paris six degrees of separation.

The house at 20 rue Jacob was built in the seventeenth
century by George Sand's great-grandfather, the soldier
Maurice de Saxe. He gave it, complete with its 'Temple
d'Amitié' in the garden, as a love token to his mistress, the
great and cultivated actress Adrienne Lecouvreur. In her
short life, Adrienne Lecouvreur was a woman as remarkable and notorious as George Sand and Colette would
become. She had many lovers. Voltaire was probably one
of them. He adored her and, along with Maurice de Saxe,
was by her side when she died.

Natalie Barney knew about the romantic history of her
house when she leased it. She, like George Sand, had a
taste for an older Paris, a Paris of romantic associations.
And, like George Sand, she was generous, placid and
romantically ruthless. She once made separate dates with
eighteen women for one night. She used to say: *I love my
life . . . I never act except according to my pleasure.* It's a stirring

echo of George Sand's wilful declaration: *Because I want it. That said everything.*

I head to the river, turning my back on the Left Bank of Paris, where the landscape binds up and subsumes all contradictions: saints and sinners, good and bad, society and individual, Christian and pagan. It's as if the tensions of these opposing forces are forever constrained by the stones and the buildings and the enduring trees. And then there are the women who confronted these tensions, who found their own ways through them and beyond them. Who always rejected death and sacrifice in favor of life and art.

When Colette died in 1954, she was the most famous and revered writer in France. She was given a State funeral, the first time a woman had been so honored. And yet the Catholic Church refused to send a priest to preside at the funeral. Graham Greene sent a famous letter of protest – and tribute – from across the Channel, explaining, *A writer whose books we love becomes for us a dearly loved person.*

Several hundred years earlier, when Adrienne Lecouvreur died in the house bought for her by George Sand's ancestor, the Church refused to give the actress a Christian burial. Like Colette, she had simply broken too many taboos. Voltaire protested, another male writer composing a passionate tribute to an artist he loved: *This incomparable actress, who almost invented the art of speaking to the heart . . .*

I hug all these thoughts to my heart, and my jacket more warmly around my chest, as I head back to the river and home.

⚜

A few hours later Rachel and I are shrugging off our coats in the doorway of Chez Omar, a restaurant on the rue de

Bretagne. It's close to Rachel's place and convenient and cheap. 'It's also fashionable, don't ask me why,' says Rachel, as we survey the high-spirited crowd.

This shabby room toned in mustard and wood does seem an unlikely fashion hangout. Far from being glamorous, it's warm and gently lit. Our host is Omar, a dapper old gentleman, whose shrewd eastern gaze rests upon us.

'This is my friend Lucinda,' says Rachel, hugging my arm. 'She's a writer, from Australia.'

'I have many clients from Australia,' says Omar in softly accented English. 'Do you know John Waters, the singer? He always comes here. And the designer, Collette . . .'

'Dinnigan,' I say. 'Yes, I know them. Well no, I don't know them, actually. But I know *of* them.'

Rachel and I stand at the bar waiting for our table as we sip a tepid *kir*. Rachel is telling me about the latest conference she has been invited to address: she is leading the intellectual argument in favor of global free trade, she is proving – bravely, methodically, logically – that third-world poverty can only be eradicated if wealthy nations like France open their trading doors. It's a message that many people don't feel inclined to hear. I feel proud to be her friend.

Omar suddenly walks back down the bar to us. He looks across the wooden counter directly at me. He is fractionally shorter.

'I would like to take you to lunch on Sunday.'

Rachel and I both know that Rachel is not included in this invitation.

'Well,' I say. This is something new. 'Ah,' I reply, 'well, that's very kind, let me think about it.'

Omar nods calmly, and then he shows us to our table. It's hard to surprise Rachel, but Omar has done it.

'Christ, you get along here much more than I do. Have you thought about moving to Paris for a while, it suits you!'

'Never. I'd find it even harder than you do. You need to be here for your work. I love visiting Paris, but I couldn't live here, you know that. I'm bound hand, foot and heart to Sydney.'

We hunch shoulders and bump elbows with the stylish young things, we eat average couscous and lamb, we speak loudly over the cheerful noise.

Rachel says, 'You should go to lunch, Lu, it's part of the Paris experience. You are a writer, they respect that here you know.' And, she adds, wanting to clarify, not wanting to be unkind, 'Perhaps Omar thinks you'll write about him and his restaurant.'

On the way out, Omar helps us into our coats and I accept his invitation. We agree to meet here on Sunday at 12:15.

As a gust of outdoor air hits our faces, Omar says softly, like a poem, like a gift, 'I like you. It seems to me that you are ready for anything.'

Like the cool wind, the remark tingles. As if this stranger sees something in me that I don't yet see myself.

❧ 9 ❧

The Language of Love

The day one sets foot in France, you can take it from
me, PURE happiness begins. Of course it's partly that
dear dear Colonel, but I don't see him all the time by
any means & every minute of every day is bliss & when
I wake up in the morning I feel as excited as if it were
my birthday.

Nancy Mitford

EVEN AS A SCHOOLGIRL I knew a secret about Nancy
Mitford. I knew she was more than just one of the
scandalous aristocratic Mitford sisters; more than just
the minor writer of comedies of manners, certainly more
than just the pen-friend of the major writer Evelyn
Waugh. In my heart of hearts I knew she was a philosopher. I worked this out by myself, as a grimy teenager
reading Penguin paperbacks on the daily bus ride home.

As the bus bumped its way through the traffic, every
now and then I would lift a blurry gaze from the printed
pages to the passing chicken shops and car yards. But all

I could see was another place and time – one in which women ruled the salons with wit and style; men loved conversation and art; and a life dedicated to pleasure was both possible and admirable.

Of course, in those days I didn't have the faintest real understanding about the source of Nancy Mitford's philosophy, but if anyone had cared to ask, I could readily have listed some of its qualities. Beauty. Pleasure. Irreverence. Worldliness. Notions far removed from the self-denying belief systems of my convent-school.

Nancy Mitford represented the entirely radical idea that life wasn't automatically about suffering and sacrificing, or even about working and acquiring. She had described a way of living which transformed daily life into an art form. She had described an *art of living*. And that, of course, is where Paris would come in.

One of these days, I thought, as the bus lurched off from the traffic lights, I'll find out about all this.

⚜

In Nancy Mitford's fictional world, the realization of every girl's dreams lies in Paris. All her best heroines find their destinies there. There's Linda of *The Pursuit of Love* and Grace of *The Blessing*. Even the prosaic Fanny ends up in Paris as wife to the British Ambassador in *Don't Tell Alfred*. And here's me, an Australian girl who has come to Paris. I'm not looking for love, however. I'm looking for Nancy Mitford.

I am wandering down Nancy Mitford's street, rue Monsieur (which she variously referred to as rue Mr or Mr St) in the discreet 7th *arrondissement*, the noble Faubourg Saint-Germain. I stand outside the bland court-yard walls of number 7. I can see the Eiffel Tower over one shoulder and the glowing dome of Louis XIV's Invalides over the other. The Musée Rodin is just down the road. The Pagoda, a Chinese-style cinema on the corner, strikes an eccentric note. The Faubourg Saint-Germain grew up in the late seventeenth and eighteenth centuries as the aristocrats moved out of the Marais district to be nearer the road to Versailles and the Sun King, Louis XIV. This neighborhood's high, discreet walls don't invite tourists to linger. There are no bustling cafés or cozy bistros. At the apex of Parisian tradition, exclusion and discretion, this *quartier* is quiet and austere.

Except to me, because even this silent courtyard door speaks loudly of Nancy Mitford. Behind this door is an eighteenth-century pavilion. Nancy Mitford lived from 1947 to 1967 in the ground floor apartment leading onto the courtyard. I know from photographs and descriptions that the apartment was neither large nor grand, but furnished with a few fine screens, antiques and fresh flowers. Here Nancy Mitford wrote her books and letters, wearing her Dior dresses and a small string of pearls, slender and upright, holding a long pen and inscribing with a clear, square hand. She was a single working woman and, though she eschewed such a pretentious term, she was an artist. Sometimes the local children played loudly in the courtyard, breaking her concentration. Sometimes her eyes hurt and she had to put down her pen. And often her friends rang her up to gossip – they too were a distraction. As if to bring the past to life, the courtyard doors momentarily draw open, and a group of pretty French children spill onto the street, laughing and shouting. I glimpse the cobblestones and the white windows before the doors are drawn closed and the street falls silent again.

These courtyard gates opened to welcome an astonishing array of guests. Evelyn Waugh was a regular visitor. Anthony Eden, Clive Bell, Cecil Beaton, Noel Coward, sister Diana Mosley and numerous French aristocrats and intellectuals all came by. Nancy entertained with small dinner parties and lunches. But though she had a hectic social life, her letters make it clear that she also spent much of her time alone. If her maid, Marie, wasn't there to cook for her, she didn't eat a thing – she boasted that she couldn't even boil an egg for herself.

I am staring blindly at the courtyard gates when a dapper old gentleman in cap and slip-on shoes strolls past me and stops.

'Are you looking for something?'

'Well, um, yes,' I fumble. 'Or rather, someone. I believe Nancy Mitford lived here?' Monsieur tilts his cap cautiously. 'She was an English writer,' I add.

'Well,' he says, in a practiced way, 'I know the film star who lives up there. See the second floor? And one of our greatest historians lived just down there. Just at the end of the street, can you see? That's where Lamartine lived.' For a moment he looks cross. 'What did this English lady write about?'

'She wrote about love,' I reply.

'Ah.' He smiles, pleased. 'Here is a story about love. You saw the beautiful *Pagode* on the corner. (Yes, Nancy refers to it in her letters, it was her local cinema.) 'It was built by Monsieur Boucicaut, the proprietor of Au Bon Marché [the department store]. He was very much in love with his wife, a beautiful and fashionable woman. She craved a Chinese pagoda. Why? It didn't matter. Unable to resist her whims, he had it built for her. It took months. But as soon as it was built she ran away with another man, breaking his heart.'

He pauses for effect. 'It was a love story, but so sad, so sad . . .' Then he tilts his cap again and ambles away down the quiet street.

⚜

Love was Nancy Mitford's business. She wrote three books with that word in the title: *Love in a Cold Climate, The Pursuit of Love* and *Voltaire in Love.*

Love in Nancy Mitford's world breaks all kinds of taboos. There's Linda's love affair with Fabrice: he won't marry her and sets her up as his mistress. Or Grace's love affair with Charles-Edouard: he sleeps around and visits one of his mistresses for 'tea' every day. Then there's Cedric, the gay Canadian, who emerges as the true heroine of *Love in a Cold Climate.* By the end of the novel Cedric has established a *ménage à trois* with Lady Montdore and Boy Dougdale.

Nancy Mitford's non-fiction lovers had even stranger love lives. Louis XV's official mistress, Madame de Pompadour, didn't particularly like sex, so Louis established a personal brothel to service him sexually. And Voltaire's love affair with Emilie de Châtelet ended with her dying in childbirth to another man while Voltaire was sending love letters to his own niece. (You call this Love? *Why not!* responds Nancy Mitford.)

The great love of Nancy Mitford's own life was a Frenchman, Gaston Palewski. She was forty-two years old and unhappily married when they met in war-time London. After the war she threw over her life and moved to Paris to be near him. He was the prototype for her characters Fabrice and Charles-Edouard – a clever, vain, elusive man. When Palewski refused to marry Nancy Mitford, she told herself at first that it was because she was married, but after her divorce it became clear that Palewski simply wasn't in love with her. So she became one of his several mistresses, and their affair followed the usual pattern: she relegated all other friendships to second place; she refrained from overt gestures of affection in public; and she arranged her timetable to his convenience. This went on for years, surviving Palewski's marriage in 1969 to a French aristocrat and continuing right up until her death in 1973.

If I had a friend who was proposing to live her life the way Nancy Mitford lived hers, I would feel obliged to give her a strong sister-to-sister talking to about wasting her life on a no-good, two-timing, low-down, absolute and utter bastard who didn't deserve her.

But, if my friend were like Nancy Mitford, nothing I could say would make a gram of difference. Nancy Mitford was well aware what people thought, and she couldn't have cared less. She wrote to Evelyn Waugh: *I suppose you think I'm a whore & my immortal soul is in danger. About once a week, for a few minutes it worries me that you should think so.*

Nancy accepted her status as the second-string mistress of a philandering Frenchman. But most of her friends couldn't. They assumed that she had a sad romantic flatness in her life, concealed under the champagne fizz of her writing. I suspect they were wrong.

In life, it seems to me, there are few things more mysterious to us than other people's romantic relationships, except possibly our own. Nancy's relationship with Palewski astounded people to the end, and after. Her sister Diana said: *She had a very happy full life, but the only thing that went wrong in her life really, was the men in it. They were hopeless.*

Nancy Mitford was clearly not a woman of her times, but nor was she ahead of her times. She was a classicist. The traditions she looked to were pre-Romantic. That's why she wrote biographies of eighteenth-century figures like Voltaire and Madame de Pompadour. She rejected the notion of modern romantic love, with its anti-social tendencies, individualistic narcissism, bourgeois emphasis on marriage and children, climactic highs and inevitable lows. She wanted to celebrate classical love – love which, at its best, was sober, understated, unsentimental and deep, and absolutely unrelated to marriage or children.

Here is an excerpt from *The Blessing*. The very English Grace has just been introduced to her French in-laws, including Charles-Edouard's grandmother.

'Who is the old man?'

'M. de la Bourlie? He's my grandmother's lover.'

'Her lover?' Grace was very much startled. 'Isn't she rather old to have a lover?'

'Has age to do with love?' Charles-Edouard looked so much surprised that Grace said, 'Oh well – I only thought. Anyway, perhaps there's nothing in it.'

He roared with laughter, saying, 'How English you are. But M. de la Bourlie has visited my grandmother every single day for forty-six years, and in such a case you may be sure that there is always love.'

Nancy Mitford snatched this lovely scene straight from history.

In 1662, the ageing duc de La Rochefoucauld fell in love with the youthful Madame de Lafayette. Until his death in 1680, every day he climbed the great hill on the Left Bank from rue Bonaparte to rue Vaugirard to visit his mistress. In Madame de Lafayette's cozy salon they pored over his maxims, and refined her novella of passion, *La Princesse de Clèves*, which Nancy Mitford would translate into English three hundred years later. The couple never displayed affection in public or gave the least sign of their attachment to each other. But they spent every day together. One of their friends, Madame de Sévigné's cousin, Bussy-Rabutin, remarked of their relationship: *In such cases there is always love, and even when old age has intervened there is still something left which, in the eyes of the Church, is as inadmissible as love itself.*

This story was very important to Nancy Mitford; she told it many times as fact and fiction. To her it signalled the perfection of the classical love story. There must have been a deep resonance for her in La Rochefoucauld's opinion that *Good marriages do exist, but not delectable ones.*

Nancy Mitford was diagnosed with Hodgkin's disease shortly after relocating to Versailles in 1967. The disease meant years of excruciating pain and multiple operations. As her illness advanced, she stopped receiving most visitors, preferring to conduct her friendships by letter. Gaston Palewski was one of the few whom she saw.

One morning her lover of nearly thirty years had a sudden and overwhelming intuition. He hurriedly made the trip from Paris to Versailles, and arrived just as Nancy was falling into unconsciousness. He sat beside Nancy and took her hand. He thought he saw her smile. He was the last person to see her before her death.

It was a fitting end to her own entirely classical romance.

As I wander down rue Monsieur, the old man returns on the other side. We bow and smile to each other as we pass by.

❧

'We are going to a house,' says Rachel emphatically, 'a *house*. Why are these people dressed for a hiking trip to the wilderness?'

Rachel and I are on the train to Versailles, and frankly, this is not an inspiring start to the trip. The Americans look appalling. What is it with microfiber tracksuits and huge sports shoes?

'Maybe they think they'll need a helicopter rescue,' I say, 'and it'll be easier to pick them out in those fluoro-colors.'

'And why,' asks Rachel, 'do they need great hulking backpacks with supplies for a month?'

I once read an article about Tom Cruise and Nicole Kidman in the early days of their famous and golden marriage. In a gesture of extreme romanticism, one that had a Hollywood *Roi Soleil* kind of grandeur about it, Tom Cruise acquired Versailles for a day. According to the reports, the beautiful couple wandered hand-in-hand through the gardens and the château. Alone, untroubled. No queues, no hawkers, no backpacks blocking their view. Just their radiant orthodontic perfection and the glories of Versailles. I remember feeling a bitter pang both at their privileged access to beauty and history, and, snobbishly, peevishly, at their ignorant unworthiness of it.

But now I wonder: what could those two possibly have thought of it all? The main château at Versailles is, I think, rather a disappointment at first. It's far less grand than you expect. And there are certainly prettier places in Paris it-self – the Hôtel de Soubise for example, in the Marais, gives you a far better sense of aristocratic seventeenth-century living. As you wander Versailles you feel rather disconcerted by the empty rooms, the cracked mirrors, the uneven layout. In the main château at least, there isn't the parade of revolution-provoking excess that the visitor secretly craves.

The thing is, Versailles unpeopled makes no sense. The whole point of Versailles was the crowd. The soldiers, the courtesans, the nobles, the gawking foreigners, the aspirants, the supplicants. Like Tom and Nicole, the *Roi Soleil* needed an audience. I think about this as we pass the African hawkers at the gate, and the busloads of Germans, and the hiking Americans. All the world came to Versailles to pay homage to the aura of power around the Sun King. All the world still does.

This time, however, Rachel and I aren't going to do the regular tour. Three days ago I rang and organized for us to attend a tour of *Les Petits Appartements de Louis XV* or, as we gleefully referred to them, the mistresses' rooms. The voice I spoke to was very polite and very competent. I was careful to make sure I understood what she said and to make myself understood in return. I *may* have asked her one time too many to repeat dates and times to be sure that I had got it right. But on the whole I thought my French wasn't too bad. Not too bad at all.

Evidently she didn't agree.

'Madame, I assure you that all conversation will be in French. There will be NO opportunity for discussion of any kind whatsoever at all in English.'

'OK,' I said.

'You will follow the tour exactly as instructed.'

'OK,' I said.

'There will be no opportunity for you to ask any questions.'

'OK,' I said. *Gee.*

At the entrance it's not hard to spot our group. The men and women are on average five kilos lighter than the hikers. The women wear light trench-coats and scarves, with sensible court shoes and handbags. Their hair is shiny, short and neat. The men all wear tailored jackets. Rachel and I have found ourselves among the French *bourgeoisie*, practical, sober, nicely cut. Our tour guide is another refined and solemn French woman. We sidle up behind them as our tour begins: mortified by my telephonic rebuke, Rachel and I are determined to blend into the group just as neatly as two slices in a baguette basket.

Our first stop is an engraving of the famous Ball of the Clipped Yew Trees, where the King seduced Jeanne, Madame d'Etioles, later Madame de Pompadour. The ball took place, we are told, in February 1745, when Jeanne was just twenty-four years old. For this masked ball the King devised a unique romantic ploy. He and seven other men covered their heads in tall masks, shaped like clipped yew trees. Everyone knew the King was under one of these ridiculous masks, bobbing loftily around the ballroom, but it was impossible to tell which one. While one of his fellow conspirators kept a hopeful Duchesse conspicuously engaged, the King dashed into the corner with the pretty and accomplished Madame d'Etioles. It was the beginning of the love affair that lasted until she died twenty years later.

I smile, at the solemn rendition as much as at the absurd tale. Rachel chuckles as she examines the engraving. But the rest of the group merely nods gravely. A kingly romance, even conducted under a tree mask two feet high, is apparently no laughing matter.

Now we head up the stairs to *Les petits appartements*. We

wander through a series of small and charming rooms, and rooms within rooms, which are clearly made for living, not posing. There's lovely gold and white wood panelling and gilded fireplaces and a golden parquet floor. Here and there we see pieces of furniture, reminders of the exquisite artistry of the period. A table of black lacquer and gilt, inlaid with delicately colored birds on the tip of flight. An oyster silk chair covered with roses. A vase as fresh-minted as a bunch of flowers. With la Pompadour installed here, this became the new heart of Versailles, with a traffic jam of art dealers, philosophers, travellers, artists, architects and craftsmen, musicians and messengers crowding into la Pompadour's cozy and intimate rooms. Every now and then the King would turn up and everyone would bow deeply and scurry off, only to return later. The duc de Cröy expected to disapprove of the bourgeois mistress, but came away enchanted: *I found her charming, both in looks and character; she was at her* toilette *and couldn't have been prettier.* Voltaire, whom Pompadour was instrumental in appointing to the lucrative and influential positions of court historian and gentleman-in-ordinary to the King, concluded that: *It was more profitable to say four words to a king's mistress than to write a hundred volumes.*

Our French guide tells about La Pompadour's magical life at court with the tidy sobriety of a Sunday school mistress. The group nods and rests its chin thoughtfully on its hand.

From la Pompadour's we move on to Madame du Barry's rooms. Contemporaries sometimes called La Pompadour a whore, but Madame du Barry was the real thing. She was well known in Paris and counted several members of the court among her clients. Legend has it that the jaded Louis XV caught sight of Jeanne du Barry in 1768 in the Hall of Mirrors. When summoned to meet him she did the unthinkable – she gave a deep curtsy and then kissed the King on the lips, smiling roguishly out of her hooded aqua eyes.

As we stroll through her rooms our guide acknowledges Madame du Barry's low beginnings, but assures us that Madame du Barry became a woman of considerable culture and refinement, adding her own luster to the glories of France. The group nods in grave agreement. But the evidence suggests otherwise.

We see the small but elaborate library, to discover that its only purpose was to disguise the secret doorway to the King's staircase. We see Jeanne's tiled English-style bathroom where she spent hours and which provides a clue to her beauty: while all the other courtiers were powdered and puffed and perfumed, she was simply, radiantly clean. Golden blonde hair, milk and roses complexion, and most of all, those eyes. One English visitor to the court said simply of the new mistress: *Her eyes are of a lively light blue and she has the most wanton look in them that I ever saw.*

Then we come across a long reclining statue. It's a full-length nude of Madame du Barry in white marble. As she lies there in her glass case on a black gilded base, Louis XV's mistress appears rather like a pornographic Snow White. Her jutting breasts, her turning bottom, her curving hip . . . even the marble fabric which winds around her body seems sinuous and erotic. True to form, our tour group murmurs solemnly as it walks past the case. Not a hint of a knowing smile, no risqué comments, not even an admiring glance at the superb physical confidence of the subject or the beauty of the marble form.

I want to say something to Rachel. Trying to ascribe to Madame du Barry the same level of culture as Madame du Pompadour would be foolish. She was a poor girl, a vulgar girl. She knew nothing about art, or architecture or culture. She didn't read serious books or play music like La Pompadour. Why pretend she did? And yet, she was an uncommonly kind and decent person. All the records show that you could count on Madame du Barry's tender heart and her gift for friendship.

And still our group retains its earnest demeanor.

It's a cliché that Australians are irreverent about our history. But it's true that we lack a certain awe. After all, our national story is brief, makeshift, often brutal and somewhat inconclusive. If we didn't laugh about it, we'd probably cry. It must be very different to be French. There's that long and complex history to sustain, the grand national narrative to be nourished and fortified. For the sake of *la gloire*, it seems that even naughty Madame du Barry must be made respectable.

As the tour comes to an end, Rachel and I finally let down our guard. We are about to giggle and nudge each other, when, to our surprise, a member of the tour group approaches us.

'You are the Australian student, no?' she says, in English.

'Yes,' I say.

'My name is Professor Verdy. We spoke on the phone.'

She smiles, and I suddenly see the good humor in her soft brown eyes. I realize now she's been watching Rachel and I behave ourselves.

'Thank you so much,' we say. 'It was wonderful, fascinating.'

'When you come to Versailles next time, ring me,' she says. 'Come again.'

It's a curious thing, the charm of the French woman. The reserve, the coolness, and then the unexpected surge of warmth.

❧

The French language, they say, is the language of love. And the tradition persists that the French are a romantic people, the world's greatest lovers. But that's not entirely true, or at least, not in the way people think. After all, this is a race that has more words for 'working girl' than any other language I know; each one, as Janet Flanner, the *New Yorker*'s 1930s Paris correspondent, observed, 'a precise professional rating'. There's *cocotte, horizontale, grisette, demi-mondaine, courtisane, demi-castor, dégrafée, irregulière, femme galante* . . .

At some stage, disconcertingly, the definitions blur, and common prostitutes at the bottom of the ladder become revered courtesans at the top. The King's favorite courtesan was the most important, soaring to the top of the social ladder with the title of *maîtresse en titre* or official mistress. I must say the step-by-step progress from whore up to mistress gets you thinking about an affair with a married man in quite a different way.

If anything, there's a deeply pragmatic aspect to French erotic culture. This is the nation that is not fazed by the fact that President Faure died while making love with his mistress in La Pompadour's former Paris home, the Élysée Palace, in 1898. Or that President Mitterrand was mourned at his State funeral in 1996, not only by his wife, but also by his mistress and love child. The greatest courtesans are affectionately memorialized. La Pompadour is remembered in the grandeur of the Pompadour Salon in the Hôtel Meurice in Paris. Jeanne du Barry, always second best, is recalled, carnally, in the Comtesse du Barry gourmet charcuterie and food supplier.

Then of course, there are legions of artworks celebrating the whore. Puccini's *La Bohème* was based on Henri Murger's novel of 1830s Paris bohemia, *Scènes de la vie de Bohème*. Mimi, the heroine, was a consumptive *grisette* who gave herself for love as much as money. There was the exquisite, also consumptive, courtesan Marguerite Duplessis, immortalized by Alexandre Dumas fils as *La Dame aux Camélias,* and later by Verdi as *La Traviata.*

Colette's novels *Chéri* and *Gigi* are a tribute to the *belle époque* courtesans, like La Belle Otéro and Liane de Pougy. Colette always liked the healthy avaricious types, the survivors. Once, during Colette's music hall days La Belle Otéro took her aside and said to her: *'You look a bit green, my girl. Don't forget that there is always a moment in a man's life, even if he's a miser, when he opens his hand wide . . .' 'The moment of passion?' 'No. The moment when you twist his wrist.'*

Perhaps the French attitude to sex is best summed up in Nancy Mitford's *The Blessing,* when a Frenchwoman speaks to an American: *'Well then, perhaps you can tell us,'* said Madame Rocher, *'how in a country where there are no brothels, do the young men ever learn?'*

According to my friend Angie, whose sampling of men is truly global, there is definitely a sound basis to the Frenchman's reputation. The best lover of all, she said, was Frédéric in Vietnam.

'Tell me why.'

'He was . . . erotic,' she said. 'Before then, I never liked doing it to music, but he did, and he made sex seem like a dance. And then he talked.'

'Talked?'

'You know, said things. During sex,' she said, adding inconsequently, 'Both his parents were psychoanalysts.'

'He said things,' she went on. 'And it was . . .' her voice took on a dreamy tone, 'erotic. And then at the end he did what no man has ever done before or since . . .'

'What?'

'He said, "'Ave you 'ad enough?"'

'Ooh,' I said, impressed but rather confused. 'And so . . . had you?'

She looked at me indignantly. I changed the question. 'Was he marvelous?'

'He was an utter bastard,' she said vehemently. 'Turned out he was sleeping with half of Hanoi, including an exquisite Vietnamese prostitute. But he was . . . erotic.'

I'm thinking about love and romance and passion and pragmatism an hour or so later as Rachel and I present ourselves at 4 rue d'Artois, also in Versailles. Here is Nancy Mitford's final home. The house she bought to die in. It's very modest: a long and narrow white house, angled to let the sun in. Here's the plaque – I've seen a photo of the occasion when it was unveiled, with Nancy's sisters standing glumly around in black. Now the plaque is looking a bit faded and unkempt, as if no one is very interested in it anymore. We walk around the back. There's a school next door where very young children are playing. In Nancy's garden the sun shines gently on waving grass and spring blossoms and chestnut candles.

'It's all a bit sad isn't it,' says Rachel.

'No,' I say defensively.

The role of the mistress is often vulnerable and painful. And lonely. But for a woman like Nancy, it would be unfair to suggest that she didn't have a choice or say in the matter; that she didn't, at some level, choose her relationship and its progress. As Nancy's sister Diana wisely said: *I suppose she wanted to marry him . . . but if she had I don't think it would have worked out . . . I think she was perfect by herself.*

In 1949 Nancy Mitford wrote to a friend: *He* [Evelyn Waugh] *has been too terrible about my book* [Love in a Cold Climate] *but the publishers are preparing for it to be another best seller & I confess that for me is what matters, so that I can go on living here – all I care about. Evelyn said it could have been a work of art – yes but I'm afraid it's here & now & the Colonel I care for.*

It may sound shallow to gloat about a prospective best-seller, but Nancy was not. In those days she was still working hard for the financial freedom to create an independent life, to make it possible to enjoy 'the here and now' and the love affair that was so important to her. Nancy Mitford's move to Versailles, was, I think, the ultimate statement of her classical values. That's why she moved to the city of aristocrats, to the home of the warrior class that went to war on behalf of France and dedicated itself devotedly to pleasure the rest of the time.

The funny thing is, *Love in a Cold Climate* did turn out to become a work of art. And Nancy did go on living in France, all the way to her death. And out of her accumulated 'heres and nows', she made a beautiful life.

⚜

Nancy Mitford wrote about all kinds of love, but there was one love experience which eluded her. Motherhood.

At first she fully expected to follow the usual path. In 1938 she wrote to a friend: *I am in the family way isn't it nice. But . . . don't tell anybody . . . it may all come to nothing.*

I am awfully excited though. She subsequently suffered a miscarriage.

In November 1941, Nancy wrote to her sister: *Darling Diana, Thank you so much for the wonderful grapes, you are really an angel & grapes are so good for me. I have had a horrible time, so depressing because they had to take out both my tubes & therefore I can never now have a child.* Nancy immediately minimized her grief: *I can't say I suffered great agony but quite enough discomfort – but darling when I think of you & the 18 stitches in your face* [due to a car accident] *it is absolutely nothing.*

Eight years later there was a curious exchange of letters between Evelyn Waugh in England and Nancy Mitford in Paris. In January 1949 she wrote joyously to her old friend: *I am having a lovely life – only sad that heavenly 1948 is over . . .* He wrote back sourly: *What an odd idea of heaven. Of course in my country we cannot enjoy the elegant clothes & meals & masquerades which fill your days . . .* In his letter Evelyn Waugh did not refer or allude in any way to Nancy Mitford's childlessness.

Yet she inferred the criticism. *Darling Evelyn, Don't be so cross & don't tease me about not having children, it was God's idea, not mine. Do you really think it's more wrong to live in one place than another, or wrong to go to fancy dress parties?*

I've thought a lot about this exchange. Evelyn Waugh was criticizing Nancy Mitford for being happy. That much is clear. *How dare you be happy!* is his unmistakeable implication. Her defense was simply that she couldn't have children, and so it was necessary to find other joys and pleasures in life. Pleasures that might appear entirely frivolous to the eyes of a devout Catholic father of a large brood. But it wasn't fair to blame her for flourishing despite the absence of children in her life.

I think a lot of women today, perhaps unconsciously, share Evelyn Waugh's view that a woman is not complete unless she has children – or, to put it another way, that a woman without children is not a true woman, but floating, anchorless and without purpose.

Many of the women I admire never had children. Nancy Mitford. Edith Wharton. Madame du Deffand. Coco Chanel. Others did but children played only a minor role in their lives. Hortense Mancini abandoned her four young children when she fled from her husband. Madame de Pompadour had a daughter with whom she spent very little time after she began her liaison with a King. Colette had a daughter with her second husband – but sent her away to be raised, only spending time with her during summer holidays. Napoleon's Josephine, by contrast, was a devoted mother of two: she died in the loving arms of her son. Yet none of these women defined themselves by their status as mothers. Nor did they expect that the experience of motherhood would completely fulfil them.

People talk a lot nowadays about *having it all*. Having the husband, having the career, having the children. And there's a cruel implication that missing out on any of these experiences is necessarily a permanent blight on life itself. Like most of us, however, Nancy Mitford didn't have it all. She graciously accepted that it just didn't work out like that. She merely had whatever was hers to have. And she made the most of it.

∾ 10 ∾

Dressed by Dior

There is no pulse so sure of the state of a nation as its characteristic art product which has nothing to do with its material life. And so when hats in Paris are lovely and french and everywhere then France is alright.

Gertrude Stein

I DON'T QUITE KNOW how to say this. *I'd like a French manicure please?* But do the French call it a French manicure? What if it's like condoms: the English called them French letters and the French call them *capotes anglaises?*

I'm in the Guerlain manicure room on the Champs-Élysées. One minute I was on the hot wide street, the next I was climbing the creaky wooden staircase to a different century, up, up and my nose twitching as I inhaled the distinctive dusty smell. Now I'm perched awkwardly on a high faded settee among stuffed chairs. Dowdy women in gilt frames are looking down their considerable noses at me. A collection of vintage Guerlain perfume bottles in a glass case adds to the historic micro-climate. Even the sunlight seems old and musty as it filters through the high windows.

Into the room walks a brusque little woman who wheels over a trolley and sets herself up in front of me. She takes her time. Only when she is quite ready does she look up and say calmly, 'Bonjour, Madame.'

Clearly, this is no fancy Sydney salon where they wrap you in blankets and burn calming oils and play new-age music, as if you are a particularly dangerous inmate in a progressive asylum. Here in Paris, beauty isn't therapy, it's business.

French polish, it's called. It takes a long time. First there's the undercoat to cover the whole nail in pink-tinged clear varnish. Then another coat, the same. Wait for it to dry. Then there's a fiddly bit where a hard white varnish is applied just to the crescent tip of the nail. My manicurist is clearly an expert though; she attacks the task with complete confidence. Wait while this dries. Then clear varnish the whole nail several times until it sets completely hard. So the crescent tips of your nails are whiter than white, and your cuticles are pink and healthy. The effect is one of heightened reality: everything looks natural, only much better, natural in a way that poor old nature could never hope to achieve.

Somehow this seems to me very French, and sets me wondering whether I am wise to be sporting this very hard red lipstick, a color which bears absolutely no relationship to nature.

My manicurist is coming to the end of her task. My hands are soft and smooth; my nails are shining. 'Now you are *soignée*,' she says, breathing a sigh of aesthetic relief. *Les petits soins* the French call it, the little attentions. In Paris, the little things matter a lot.

Possibly my favorite Hollywood film about Paris is the fifties musical *Funny Face*, which it's only fair to warn you, fails as a film largely because of the miscasting of the million-year-old Fred Astaire as the love interest to the radiant Audrey Hepburn.

Discovered by famous fashion photographer Fred as she works, mouse-like, in a dark and cavernous bookshop, Audrey is whisked to Paris for a fashion shoot. At one stage she repudiates the shallow world of fashion and sneaks off to a smoky basement where a Sartrean guru holds court. She is adorably earnest in her intellectual black stovepipe pants, skivvy and ballet shoes. But we all know it won't last. Because what she really wants to do is put on a Dior frock and twirl deliriously under the Eiffel Tower, releasing a bunch of celebratory balloons. That's what tends to happen to bookish girls in Paris: you arrive an intellectual, you depart a fashion victim.

I head down the stairs, holding my hands carefully in front of me. They look lovely.

❖

I was very disappointed the first time I walked down Avenue Montaigne. I thought it was too big. It's still too big. It's a big walk and the price tags are even bigger. This is *couture* row, and the signs say Christian Dior, Chanel, Emanuel Ungaro, Nina Ricci, Valentino . . .

Clothes are a funny business. No matter what we wear, we are saying something about ourselves to other people. If we are in fashion or out of it, expensively dressed or simply dressed, soberly or loudly or eccentrically attired – what we wear is a public message. And because we can choose what we wear in a way that we can't choose our eye color or height, our clothes go beyond being a simple reflection of self to an active invention of public identity. As little girls we play dress-up, practicing being women. As women we still play dress-up, practicing being the women we want to be – or at least, be taken for.

The French understand this very well: in fact, clothes once played an important political role. At the court of Louis XIV, the nobles were classified by what they wore. The old nobility were known as the *noblesse d'épée*, the nobility of the sword. The new class of nobility was based on their juridical and administrative functions on behalf of the crown, and they were known as the *noblesse de la robe*. More generally, clothes were an all-purpose symbol of social status. The parties and balls of the court of Versailles were open to people of any rank, as long as they were dressed appropriately.

I always laugh when I read a women's magazine declaring that some starlet or other has an 'individual' or 'unique' style, when all she wears is a minute variation on prevailing fashions. In fact, all of us wear a modern uniform. And really, this is no bad thing. It's a way in which we all say that we consent to live with each other; that we accept the terms of modernity. I'm like you, our clothes say to each other, I'm with you. In many respects it's not all that different from the days of Louis XIV.

But there's one wonderful difference. Whereas in Louis XIV's day only the very rich could afford to wear the appropriate clothes, today mass production means most of us can afford some gesture towards the latest fashion, if we choose. Coco Chanel was the first designer to understand the democratization of fashion. She not only accepted this, she actively embraced it. She thought it was wonderful that her clothes were widely copied, that a shop girl could achieve the same look as a countess. *A fashion that does not reach the streets is not a fashion*, was Chanel's view, and her supreme fashion insight.

When I read the various biographies of Coco Chanel, however, I learned a few things about *haute couture*. I discovered that it is special because it combines the art of design with the craft of tailoring. Coco Chanel would fit her clothes directly on her models so that they flowed and curved with the line of their bodies. In particular, she was obsessed with the cut of the sleeve. She would cut her dresses and jackets very high under the armpit. The effect was to give a woman a lean, long torso and slender arms. At the same time she carefully shaped the sleeve so that the woman would have maximum shoulder rotation and movement. The fit was perfect both for beauty and wearability.

After reading this I looked carefully at the photos of Chanel *couture*, and then at my own suit jackets. Hmm. My clothes looked like sacks by comparison. More importantly, I looked sack-ish in them. Chanel was also remarkable because she made her clothes to last. She was still wearing the same little suits thirty years after she first made them, and they still looked beautiful. She turned fashion into anti-fashion, by making it timeless. She turned fashion into style.

Looking in the windows of these elegant stores I can still see something of the fine tailoring and detailed work that makes *haute couture* special. And insanely expensive.

Edith Wharton only wore the finest clothes. She thought that beautiful clothes were an art form. One of the things she loved most about living in Paris was that the French agreed with her. She wrote:

The artistic integrity of the French has led them to feel from the beginning that there is no difference in kind between the curve of a woman's hat-brim and the curve of a Rodin marble, or between the droop of an upholsterer's curtain and that of the branches along a great avenue laid out by Le Nôtre.

Gertrude Stein went a step further. She said:

It is funny about art and literature, fashions being part of it. Two years ago everybody was saying that France was down and out, was sinking to be a second rate power, etcetera, etcetera. And I said but I do not think so because not for years not since the war have hats been as various and lovely and as french as they are now. Not only are they to be found in the good shops but everywhere there is a real milliner there is a pretty french little hat.

It has to be admitted that, even as she was writing this, Nazi Germany was about to invade France – but then, politics was never Miss Stein's strong point.

I am not sure that high fashion can, any longer, be equated to art and literature. Today it all seems so corporatized and commercial. And yet, every now and then something magical occurs when a great artist adorns beautiful bodies with beautiful clothes. At John Galliano's 1998 show for Christian Dior at the Opéra Garnier, people simply burst into tears because the clothes and atmosphere were so exquisite.

Nancy Mitford never bothered to analyze the social function or aesthetic value of clothes. She just adored them. Most of all, she adored Monsieur Dior, whose *atelier* was here, at number 30 Avenue Montaigne. *Have you heard about the New Look?* she wrote to Eddie Sackville-West, cousin of Vita. *You pad your hips & squeeze your waist &*

skirts are to the ankle it is bliss. She wrote to her mother: *I've got a beautiful Dior dress, day, which is worn over a crinoline, I feel like a Victorian lady for purposes of loo – very inconvenient! It's so plain that I can wear it in the street & I see by the looks I get that it is a smash hit.*

After a big burst of spending on the 1951 Dior Fall collections, Nancy Mitford admitted to Evelyn Waugh:

> *I went & ordered the plainest little wool dress you ever saw from Dior £168. It's the last time. I humbly asked if they wouldn't take off the 8 but no they cried you are very lucky. All the prices are going up next week. They made me feel I'd been too clever for words. But after I felt guilty – all the poor people in the world & so on. It's terrible to love clothes as much as I do.*

Today, even with my perfectly painted fingernails, I am too frightened to try and enter Dior. I fear some unpredictable humiliation inflicted by a shop assistant. This is unfair, as normally I find French shop assistants to be extremely courteous in their remote way, although Nancy Mitford once wrote gleefully about the time two English duchesses were turned away from this very shop because *the people at the entrance considered them too dowdy to be admitted.* Clothes shopping in general is a problem for me in Paris as I am 166 centimeters tall and have hips. And breasts. French women – and the clothes designed for them – are generally petite, slim-hipped and flat-chested. The clothes are beautiful, but not for me. Now the Italians, they know how to make clothes for women with curves.

In the midst of all the grand couture windows is a tiny boutique on a sunny corner. A single rococo chandelier twinkles over the room. It's Parfums Caron. I peer in the window at the amber-filled glass flasks lined up like so many magic potions. Rachel told me that she was once asked as a favor to a friend to purchase some perfume here. She stood in front of these bottles: their names were like wishes: *N'aimez que moi* (Love no one but me!) and *French can can*. She looked at the slip of paper in her purse and indicated to the assistant, who languidly held a minuscule bottle under a tap. They watched together as tiny drops of golden syrup, *Tabac Blond*, leached into the bottle. The assistant then blandly quoted the cost. It was so unbelievably expensive that Rachel's blood began to drain from her head, only at a much faster rate than the dropping elixir. Afterwards she had to repair to the nearby Plaza Athénée for a reviving champagne. She kept checking her bag to make sure the lid of the little perfume bottle was firmly secured.

Different cultures approach the idea of personal decoration and adornment in different ways. Paris is still the center of the Western cultural ideal of feminine beauty. Women from all over the world come to Paris headquarters for a femininity infusion. Here we are all reminded of the global standard and here we undertake the necessary remedial tasks to bring ourselves back up to it: a new dress, an intake of beautiful art, long walks along the Seine, watching and being watched in a sidewalk café. Ah, yes, that's right, this is what being a woman is all about.

For an Australian woman there's another dimension to this essential Paris experience. When Australia was colonized, the notion of an ornamental woman – a woman of wit, pleasure, society – was a luxury the white colonizers couldn't afford. Women were brought to Australia as convicts and later servants. In 1800, while Napoleon's Josephine was running up dressmakers' bills and planting roses at Malmaison, and Germaine de Staël was juggling husband and lover and hosting the most influential salon in Paris, white Australian women, like the horses, and the cattle, were working and struggling just to survive.

And here's something else, something curious. Sydney today is one of the world capitals of transvestism, of men dressing extravagantly, glamorously, theatrically – and yes, monstrously – as women. My apartment complex is one of the key preparation sites for Sydney's gay and lesbian Mardi Gras: it's quite something to observe fifteen men in wigs and pink tutus posing for photographers at the end of your swimming pool. And the only Australian I know who really understands the power of makeup is a six-foot-three tranny with a skin problem. Kylie Minogue once said, witty as hell, that she thought of herself as a tall drag queen in a short woman's body. It's as if we Australian women missed our chance to be the decorative sex in Australia – and the men have mounted a takeover.

Shakespeare's women, wonderful creatures like Portia and Rosalind, dressed up as men to make men wiser, to teach them something. Like Portia revealing the quality of mercy. And this made me think in a different way about the Australian drag scene. And about Dame Edna Everage, Barry Humphries's grotesque and compelling alter-ego. And even about Patrick White, whose late work *The Twyborn Affair* is not just about transvestism, but a poetic exploration of the relationship between our external appearance and our internal identity. Perhaps it's not too far-fetched to wonder if Australian men dress as women to teach women something?

I quite enjoy my ruminating walk down Avenue Montaigne, but to me it's not really about the essence of French femininity. The fashionable women I see along the street are mostly foreigners. There is a slightly desperate look about their wobbling ankles. The really nice thing about

French style is that many French women aren't compet-
ing in the impossible and expensive race that is modern
fashion. They tend to avoid the dramatic ups and downs
of hemlines, the ins and outs of pant widths, the fads for
stilettos or acid green or torn sleeves or corset belts.

I am too timid to enter Mr Dior's shop, and the truth is
I don't particularly want to, though I am glad to know it's
there. I'm rather like Gertrude Stein, who, judging by the
photos, wore a tent for twenty years, but still admired
fashion as an art form. *Fashion*, she said, *is the real thing in
abstraction.*

The French also understand that clothes aren't everything. Josephine Baker arrived in Paris from the poorest
southern region of the U.S., via bit parts in vaudeville on
Broadway. She came to Paris armed only with her magnificent ebony body, a comic genius and the very good
advice of the French waiters she met in New York: *Be
chic and make them laugh!* they counselled the young per-
former.

Josephine Baker made her entry right here at 15
Avenue Montaigne, the theater of the Comédie des
Champs-Élysées. She was a minor player in a novelty show
called *La Revue Nègre* in 1925. She appeared on stage
entirely nude except for a pink flamingo feather between
her limbs. Her body, her comical gestures, her beauty were
sublime. The crowd went berserk and she became
instantly famous.

Baker was another of those women who adopted Paris
because Paris welcomed her. In America she was abused,
reviled and discriminated against. In Paris she was wor-
shipped as a stage goddess, sex symbol and a genuine artist.
I have two loves, sang Josephine Baker, *my country and Paris!*
They couldn't have been more different, yet it's nice to

think that Gertrude Stein also said, *America is my country and Paris is my home town.*

At the end of Avenue Montaigne is Pont de l'Alma, underneath which the English Princess Diana met her death. Rachel and I disagree about Diana. Rachel thinks she was a shallow publicity-seeking Sloane Ranger. I loved her, and still do. I cried when she died.

Sometimes I think of Princess Diana's last night on earth, and quite frankly, who could have had a better one? She was on holiday, having cruised around the Mediterranean on a beautiful yacht. She had just been taken to dinner at the Hôtel Ritz by a fabulously wealthy and attractive man who adored her. He had given her an enormous diamond ring as a gift. There must be many worse ways to go.

⚜

I'm at it again. I shouldn't be doing this; I know it's a weakness. But I submit to this guilty pleasure each time I come to Paris. Why? It's not as if I haven't been taught a few lessons. I have a drawer full of evidence at home in Sydney that reminds me: *Lucinda, you can't wear scarves the way French women do.* But here I am in a boutique in Place des Vosges and the old romance is reasserting itself. Oh, but this is Paris, where being a woman is special. Oh, and these scarves are works of art, richly textured and beautifully made. They are heirlooms, treasures.

The elegantly elongated saleswoman gently selects a scarf and brings it close to me. It's among the most daring; pale green silk backing an oblong of red velvet, brocade and silk. It's dramatic, almost heraldic. She carefully ties it for me, draping it across my body with strong, thin fingers.

'Comme c'est chic,' she says solemnly, standing back to appraise her handiwork. I can't help it, I preen a little.

As I hurry along the colonnades I can feel the soft weight of the scarf in its elegant shopping bag, and I already foresee its double future. In one version, I too possess that easy French elegance. I take the scarf out of the drawer and drape it across my shoulders. Even in my regulation black suit, I am lifted, lightened and irradiated. In the other future, I fling and heave, I crush and crinkle, and what looks so silken and sinuous when tied upon me by a Parisienne merely looks lumpen when adjusted by me. So it appears destined to return, carefully folded, to my drawer, where it will nestle against the other scarves I have proudly brought home from Paris. Now I see myself, standing in front of the mirror, a soulless creature in a black suit, devoid of heraldic glamor.

I don't really understand how they do it, but French women still manage to convey the impression that they've got some indefinable 'it' factor.

Consider Colette. Colette oozed a particularly French brand of feminine power. Now it needs to be understood: Colette had never been stylish. She was far too bohemian. She loved food too much to stay slim, so she got fat. She refused to wear shoes and wore sturdy leather sandals. She permed her hair so hard it stuck out from her head in a purple fizz. At one stage, mistaking her interest for exper-tise, Colette opened a beauty shop with the help of some rich supporters. As proprietor, Colette insisted that all her clients adopt her own distinctive look. Some of Paris's most famous blonde beauties emerged from Colette's salon aged immeasurably with rings of dark kohl around their eyes and fiercely blackened eyebrows. The business folded soon after.

But none of this mattered. Colette was the essential woman; she was the ultra-femme. Everyone who met her knew the legendary story of the lithe, gamine Colette whose husband, Willy, locked her in a room and urged her to write the saucy *Claudine* stories. Or the time she caused a riot by kissing her female lover on stage. And everyone had read the scandalous, captivating stories: about love between an old courtesan and a gigolo, opium dens and faked orgasms, strange *ménages à trois* and sad, cross-dressing lesbians.

When Colette was asked for guidance by aspiring writers, she always gave the same advice: *Look for a long time at what pleases you, and longer still at what pains you.* What Colette liked most was to look at women, herself included. She was a tireless and pitiless observer of the process – the business, even – of being a woman. And her observations make inspiring and sometimes excruciating reading. In *Chéri* one retired courtesan murmurs to another: '*Heavens, how good you smell. Have you noticed that as the skin gets less firm the scent sinks in better and lasts much longer? It's really very nice.*' Ouch.

Nancy Mitford greatly admired Colette. So when she was asked to translate Colette's *Chéri* for the stage, it gave her the rare opportunity to spend one hour with the great writer, who was by then a frail seventy-nine-year-old. I imagine Nancy Mitford standing in the quadrangle of the Palais Royal, smoothing down the padded skirts of her Dior day dress. She fully expects to be scrutinized by those wide, slanting, ever-observant eyes. And, of course, she wants to please Colette's eyes, to receive her feminine stamp of approval. So Nancy Mitford mounts the wooden steps, perhaps carrying her copy of *Chéri* for the great writer to sign.

Colette receives Nancy Mitford from her high divan bed pushed up against the window in the Palais Royal, in what Colette called *the heart, the very heart, of Paris*. The walls are covered in dark red silk. The shelves of the room are lined with books and busts and her collection of brightly colored glass paperweights. There's a bunch of flowers sent by an admirer. The bed is red, and a fur blanket covers Colette's arthritic and useless legs. Under the blanket, her toenails are painted scarlet. A trolley carries her work-bench with its blue lamp and pages of sky-blue paper to write on, a phone, pens, bowls of colored sweets.

Colette herself – even old, fat and infirm – is a proud lioness, with her mane of hair, her eyes rimmed with kohl, her lips stained red. And as always, she wears a patterned scarf around her neck. It's not that she is more stylish or more beautiful or more feminine than Nancy Mitford, it's that over the course of her life, she has accumulated her femininity, analyzed and endorsed it, embraced it.

The two women spend an hour together. How I wish I knew what they said to each other, the sensual bohemian and the witty aristocrat. All we know of their conversation is derived from a few brief lines that Nancy wrote to Evelyn Waugh after her meeting with Colette. Of the translation work, Nancy said little, and in the end nothing came of it. But she was overwhelmed by the privilege of meeting *Colette whom I admire more than anybody – any woman at least*. And possibly she was intimidated, a little daunted by the great dame: *I felt very shy*, she recalled. Then she added these revealing, tell-tale words: *But she admired my clothes so that was nice*. Such was the extraordinary authority of Colette, and the mystical power of the French woman.

Colette was not only charming; she understood the uses of charm. Her flattery similarly disarmed American author Anita Loos. In 1951 Loos visited Colette to talk about the stage adaptation of *Gigi*. Colette met Anita in Le Grand Véfour: Anita had prepared a little speech in tribute to the great author. She was just warming up when Colette brushed her comments aside with her hand. *Where had Anita found those adorable shoes?* Anita, of course, raced home to note down the compliment.

Thinking on these things, on the pitfalls of being in Paris and trying to wear clothes in the French manner, my confidence plummets. I privately vow not to wear my scarf in Paris, but wait until I get home to Sydney.

Then another thought: perhaps it's wisest if non-French women don't wear scarves at all. One, after all, killed American Isadora Duncan. After years of living in Paris, one day the avant-garde dancer hopped into her sportscar on the Riviera, wound a long chiffon scarf around her neck and cried, *I go to my glory!* as she sped off. Then the scarf caught in the car wheel and she strangled herself.

<e> 11 <e>

Place Vendôme

Women run to extremes; they are either better or worse than men.

La Bruyère

I T'S AN OVERCAST DAY as I stroll along rue de Castiglione towards Place Vendôme in the 1st *arrondissement*. Here, say all the guidebooks, I will confront one of the masterpieces of Paris. And last time I saw Place Vendôme I adopted the official line: it was stunning, beautiful, *god, of course!* a masterpiece. Dazzled by Paris, in awe of its grand monuments, it never occurred to me that any alternative opinion was possible.

Rachel changed all that over breakfast this morning. Face obscured behind the *International Herald Tribune*, coffee cup moving expertly from table to mouth, she scanned the latest United States political news while I looked at notes and guidebooks and planned my day which included, I added aloud, a visit to Place Vendôme and the Hôtel Ritz. As she turned the page and re-crossed her legs I suddenly heard Rachel's voice above the crackle, 'Always thought Place Vendôme was ugly.' She raised her right hand, short dark nails clashing dramatically with her Cartier tank ring, a plain gold band crested by a square golden citrine. 'That's why I bought *this* in Cartier's Left Bank store instead.' Still engrossed in American politics, she doesn't notice my astonishment at her casual heresy.

Now, as I turn from rue de Castiglione into Place Vendôme, I experience this place as if for the first time. The first thing I notice is the temperature. It starts to drop. Everything seems cold – from the blue-grey buildings set in a massive octagon, to the black unyielding asphalt which covers the huge central square. The sky itself seems lower here, a watery grey sponge pressing the slate rooftops. Squeezed up through the middle of Place Vendôme is the greenish, rusty Vendôme column: now I see that this long thin spire lacks the necessary scale and power to dominate the space.

Place Vendôme is where cold hard cash meets the beautiful things that money can buy. JP Morgan and the Banque National de Paris nestle against Cartier, Bulgari, Boucheron, Armani and Chanel. It's all very impressive, as it should be, for this square was built to impress. Here is the *Roi Soleil*'s absolute authority embodied in architecture: magnificent, orderly and harmonious. Instead of whole buildings, the architect simply designed uniform facades, giving Place Vendôme the atmosphere of a stage-set, a theater for the display of wealth and power. From an aerial view it would be exactly the same shape as a square-cut diamond – and on the ground it has the same bright cold hardness.

There are no cafés here, no garden benches, no perches to prop against and no little nooks from which to stare or daydream. So I do what all the tourists do: I crawl around the edge of Place Vendôme, looking in shop windows. I walk past the Gianmaria Buccellatti jewels and Giorgio Armani suits and Mikimoto pearls and Patek Philippe watches. Like everyone else I am reduced to making clownish ooh-aah faces as I press my face against the glass windows. A perfect suit, a string of matchless pearls, ooh, aah. My face blanches in the cold bluish reflection of diamonds.

Now I arrive at number 12, opposite the Ritz, where Chaumet jewelers displays a single magnificent necklace of rubies, pearls and diamonds. The collar rests insolently upon its velvet bed. On my reflected face I see conflicting emotions. There's admiration and awe, certainly. There's also uneasiness at the blatant excess of the gesture.

Next to the shop is an elaborate entrance to the apartments above. In October 1849 Europe's most adored Romantic composer, Frédéric Chopin, lay dying up there, in the exquisite gold and white salon of a financier's borrowed apartment. At only thirty-nine years old, he was dying, some said, of a broken heart, and all due to the woman who had been his companion for ten years, who had dumped him two years earlier by what his friend, the artist Eugène Delacroix, called *an inhuman letter*. That woman was, of course, George Sand.

A bevy of Poles and artists and society ladies walked through these heavy iron doors and climbed these curved stairs to pay homage to Chopin. An opera singer sang for him. Eugène Delacroix gently talked to him. Fashionable women flocked for the privilege and social cachet of sobbing quietly at their idol's side. Chopin, conscious and unconscious by turns, lay lightly on his death-bed. He moaned and prayed and slept and whispered. The society ladies' sobs turned to recriminations when Chopin murmured, weakly, *She said to me that I would die in no arms but hers* . . . before expiring. His love affair with George Sand had been the major relationship of Chopin's life.

You will still find Poles who have not forgiven George Sand for Chopin's early death. An old friend of Chopin's, Count Wojciech Grzymała, who knew them both well, attributed Chopin's demise directly to George Sand: *If he had not had the misfortune of meeting GS, who poisoned his whole being, he would have lived to be Cherubini's age* [that is, 82].

George Sand was well aware of the criticisms directed against her. She wrote a novel and memoir about her relationship with Chopin, portraying him as an immature and jealous child. People were amazed by her self-assurance: *The conversation this evening at the Princess's* [Princess Mathilde], *turned to Mme Sand. We discussed the question of Mme Sand's love affairs and everybody agreed that she had a very unfeminine nature, with basic coldness which allowed her to write about her lovers when practically in bed with them.*

George Sand's longest relationship was with a humble engraver, who was, she said, *as faithful as a dog.* After fifteen years of loyal service and love, Manceau died in her arms in 1865. The playwright Alexandre Dumas went to visit George Sand. With the dead man still awaiting burial, he asked her how she felt. *I feel,* she answered, *like having a bath, going for a walk in the woods and going to the theater this evening.* Dumas recounted this tale to the Goncourt brothers, concluding that Madame Sand was *a monster unconscious of her depravity, her egoism, her good-natured cruelty.*

As I continue around Place Vendôme the somber beat

of Chopin's funeral march fills my head. But quite different tunes suggest themselves when I arrive at the Chanel
boutique – some hot Sidney Bechet jazz, perhaps, or the
jangly sparkle of Stravinsky's *Le Sacre du Printemps*.

In 1929, Coco Chanel had made it. She had become
the most influential person in fashion. She had showed
women how to strip off their heavy satins and corsets,
chop off their hair and move their bodies in the sunshine
until they turned slender and golden. Then she put them
into the lightest, easiest, softest clothes. By day they wore
lithe jersey dresses or little suits; it was all short, sexy and
free. By night they wore little black dresses with delicate
beading and floating tiers and strings of translucent pearls.

One of Coco Chanel's lovers was the Duke of Westminster, the richest man in England, friend to the Prince of
Wales and the Churchills. He wooed her with jewels
hidden in posies of daisies. Chanel loved magnificent
jewels and she bought many herself, but she was the first
woman to openly mix real and costume jewelry. Though a
peasant by birth, she had a kind of aristocratic *hauteur* about
her. *The point of jewelry*, she said disdainfully, *is not to make
women look rich, but to adorn them, which is not the same thing.*

Once the Duke of Westminster was unfaithful to Coco.
Aboard his enormous yacht, cruising the Mediterranean
in luxury, he gave her a priceless pearl rope in apology. She
looked him in the eye as she held the pearls over the deck-
rail of the yacht and deliberately allowed them to slip
through her fingers into the sea. Did he ask her to marry
him? If he did, Coco later denied that she gave him this
magnificent response: *Everyone marries the Duke of Westminster. There are a lot of duchesses but only one Coco Chanel.*

On my circuit around the Place I now approach the
Ritz. When César Ritz set about designing his new hotel

in 1897 at the height of Paris's *belle époque*, he specifically planned it as a place to flatter women, to emphasize their softness, their pliability. The sweeping staircase was designed to show off the shapely curves of women making an entrance. Pink silk lampshades ensured the light would be flattering to smooth society complexions. Little hooks for handbags were situated under the custom-made restaurant chairs – they are still there today. Modern, well-lit bathrooms encouraged attention to personal hygiene.

Monsieur Ritz cultivated the delicious fiction of feminine sweetness and clean docility. It was a story only a man could have believed.

⚜

So here I am in the front bar of the Hôtel Ritz, looking out on the famous courtyard, sipping a glass of champagne, surrounded by glamorous ghosts.

Here's Coco Chanel. Her spindly frame glides past me and up the stairs to her suite on the rue Cambon side of the hotel. It's 1971, a very cold and quiet Sunday afternoon in the Christmas holiday season. She enters her suite where a fire glows and her maid, Jeanne, hovers. Coco is tired. Since bursting out of retirement in 1954, she has worked relentlessly. When she closed up her shop at the beginning of World War Two, Coco assumed her career was over. She believed that her elegant, simple clothes had permanently transformed fashion – that she had accomplished her life's mission.

But in 1947, a bald, rotund, retiring gay man named Christian Dior released his first collection – an unashamed *hommage* to *belle époque* glamor – including wasp-waists, ankle-length skirts with yards of fabric, stiletto heels and, most extraordinary of all, the return of the corset. These absurdly beautiful, impractical and feminine clothes immediately captured the war-torn and glamor-deprived hearts of fashionable women everywhere.

Chanel was horrified. She, who had meticulously crafted clothes on female bodies, was now being eclipsed by a little man who drew sketches in his bathtub. She fumed as she pored over the fashion magazines. *Ah no!* she shouted furiously, *definitely no, men were not meant to dress women!* There was only one thing to be done. Chanel would have to come back and fight the fight anew. *Once I helped liberate women, I'll do it again,* she declared.

The Americans were the first to come back to Chanel. A new generation of women was becoming liberated. They wanted clothes in which to live, work and be active. Season after season they snapped up the new Chanel classics, suits and dresses of immaculate simplicity.

Now, on this winter's afternoon, Coco is in the final stages of preparation for the Fall collections, to be shown on February 5. Her motto has always been: *There's a time for work and a time for love. That leaves no other time* . . . For Mademoiselle Chanel, the time for love has long passed, but the work has never let her down. Now, suddenly, even the work seems an unbearable burden.

Coco slips off her shoes and lies on the bed. She turns her head to look at a small icon given to her many years ago by one of her lovers, Igor Stravinsky. Suddenly Coco cries out hoarsely, *I'm suffocating!* Jeanne runs to help her, but for Coco, death is already on its way. With typical candor Coco faces her situation. *So this is how you die,* she says. These are her last words.

Now it's another winter's day, this time in February 1997. American Ambassador Pamela Harriman has swept into the hotel. This seventy-six-year-old in her power suit and gold jewelry, her body toned by exercise, her face lifted by discreet surgery, is still beautiful. She descends to the Ritz spa, a peach-colored haven complete with Roman-style frescoes and mosaics. In the soft light she lowers herself into the pool, carefully holding her radiant golden head above the water.

There was a time when Pamela Harriman came to the Ritz as a kept woman, a paid-up courtesan who catered to powerful men. These were vulnerable times, finally and wonderfully erased by a lucrative third marriage. Now she is a wealthy widow of substance. She has the grateful ear of President Clinton and the open admiration of President Chirac. The nasty lawsuit brought by her step-children finally appears to have been resolved by negotiation. And when she retires at the end of the year, she will move to her new apartment on the rue de Varenne, where, as an elegant older woman, her cosmopolitan Parisian friends will warmly welcome her.

But, all at once, as she raises and lowers her arms in the water, she feels dizzy. She slowly climbs out of the pool, and abruptly staggers and falls to the ground. Suddenly helpless, to her own surprise the fear overtakes her and she weeps. The hotel staff surround and comfort her; they call her assistant and an ambulance. Ambassador Harriman is having a massive stroke and will die that evening in hospital.

It's still 1997, a fateful year for the Ritz, but now the seasons have shifted again and it's late summer. Diana, Princess of Wales, is eating a meal in the famous dining room with her lover, Dodi Fayed. At thirty-six years old, tanned and toned, dressed simply in a dark jacket and white pants, she is beautiful. She looks like a model, but she is actually a social revolutionary. She has rejected the throne of England and has set up an alternative court – a court of public opinion – in which she plans to rule as the Queen of Hearts. After their meal, Dodi and Diana slip out the rue Cambon entrance to avoid the paparazzi. A massive car accident, less than a mile away, kills Dodi immediately; Diana dies on her way to hospital.

Sitting here in the Ritz Bar, I think of the will and determination of each of these women. Coco Chanel bursting out of retirement to save her legacy of fashion liberation. Pamela Harriman transforming herself from courtesan to Ambassador. Diana evolving from self-conscious teenager to Queen of Hearts.

And here in the Ritz each of these women spent her last waking hours. Not one of them was nice, particularly, or even good. But they were fighters, all three of them. And Paris was where they won their greatest victories.

I raise my champagne glass in silent salute. And the honeyed perfume of Chanel No. 5 rises up around me like incense.

⚜

Later I walk through heavy glass doors and along the hotel's elongated corridors. It's quiet and discreet but you can smell the money, and the power behind it. And I recall the times I made my way through Australia's own corridors of power. I would accompany the Deputy Prime Minister to meetings in Parliament House. He was a big man, with a long and anxious stride. We were always in a hurry. My heels clacked unevenly on the parquet floor as I shifted the papers and pen and mobile phone in my hands. The Minister striding in front, his adviser – hurried, deferential – behind.

But here's the crazy thing. Whenever we reached a set of heavy Parliamentary glass doors, the Minister would pull up abruptly, swing open the doors and stand chivalrously to one side as his female staff member, mortified, head down, hurried through. Then I would jump to one side so that my powerful boss could resume his long march through the House. And once again I would take up my proper place and scurry behind. We formed an antiquated double helix of power, the boss–servant relationship and the male–female one.

Wherever we were going, we almost always arrived early. One time we arrived in a sunny conference room well ahead of a Korean trade delegation. The Deputy Prime Minister was in an expansive mood. He had been meeting with a former colleague – a former premier married to a beautiful and dynamic younger wife – and relationships were on his mind.

'There's a lot of blokes who marry very young women the second time around,' he said. 'Gee, that's a lot of work. A bloke gets older and he just wants to relax.'

'But, what?' I prompted.

'But the young wives, they don't want their husbands to slow down. They think they'll turn into old men.'

'So what happens?'

'The old bloke gets bullied by his wife into taking up appointments and running inquiries and going on boards. The women get the whip out.'

I formed a rapid mental image of some old political warhorse reclining peacefully on his sunny garden deckchair, the newspaper rising and falling on his slumbering face. And then a blonde with taut features rushes out the kitchen door to lash him back into public life.

'But surely these men could just say no?' I suggested.

The Deputy Prime Minister looked incredulous. 'Oh no they couldn't,' he said.

❦

It's dusk as I emerge onto Place Vendôme, and the whole world has changed. The sky is an intense, deep blue. The sun has disappeared, but the moon and stars are not yet out. It's *l'heure bleue*. Suspended between day and night, the Place Vendôme takes on a different aspect. Its formal perfection reveals itself under the low, deep square of sky. The blue hue of the buildings deepens as the first lamps illuminate the square. I begin to understand its beauty.

Here, each day between 1878 and 1894 a woman would emerge from number 26 to take a turn in the evening air. She was draped and swathed in black veils so that no one could see her face. But everyone knew who she was: Madame La Castiglione, one-time *femme fatale*, mistress to Napoleon III and well-known narcissist, who asked photographers to produce no less than 434 portraits in tribute to her beauty. Unable to bear the demise of her looks, unable to cope with the inevitable ravages of time, she lived reclusively in her apartment in semi-darkness; the walls were painted black and mirrors were banned. Three locked doors barred the entrance. La Castiglione had defined herself by her feminine beauty alone, and when it died, then somehow her will to live died as well. She didn't have what it took to reinvent herself: she just gave up.

I leave the Place Vendôme. Ugly? Beautiful? I really don't know. But I feel its power.

12

On Grown-up Women

Compared with the women of France, the average
American woman is still in the kindergarten.

Edith Wharton

It clung in my mind like the edge of a dream as I
surfaced this morning. The sun streamed in, the curtains
lifted and swayed and I glimpsed some – if not all – of
what my journey is about. At the age of thirty-five, as
I start the rest of my life, am I not simply wondering this:
How to be? Or more exactly, how to be *as a woman*?

And surely this question is mine to explore, for was it
not first put to the world by a French woman and most
famously taken up by an Australian? Without intending to,
I find I've put myself in the footsteps of women's ideas, as
well as their lives.

Simone de Beauvoir said it in 1949: *Woman is not born,*

but made. It was one of those eureka moments when everyone slaps their forehead and says, but of course! Woman was the second sex: woman was the made-up gender. Her identity was fabricated. And the making of a woman was framed by all kinds of unjust or untested assumptions. Women were to be the mothers, the help-meets, the handmaidens. Discriminated against in work and education and society, women were constructed to be second class.

And yet, there's that ringing phrase: *Woman is not born, but made.* Today women like me have all the freedom in the world. We can decide what and who we want to be. Whether we want a capital-C career or not. Whether we want marriage. Whether we want children. We can *make* ourselves. We can decide. *I* can decide.

And here I am in Paris, the city that attracts women who want to make themselves, from Edith Wharton to Gertrude Stein. Paris is where a woman can make – or remake – herself.

And then, like a one-two punch, there's the famous follow-up question, bluntly put by a six-foot-tall Australian libertine with huge dark eyes: *What will you do?* asked Germaine Greer in concluding *The Female Eunuch.*

In liberal societies, women can do anything men can do. We can be as important or modest as any man, as brave or cowardly, as brilliant or foolish. But the thing that Paris reminds us is simply this: whatever we do, we will always be women – it's our one irreducible fact, it's our destiny, it's our responsibility to discharge.

And, I don't always think this, but right now, today, as the sun lifts the curtain on a Paris morning, I can't help thinking it's also our good fortune.

❧

There's a plaque to Edith Wharton outside her house in 53 rue de Varenne, one of the most exclusive locations in the Faubourg Saint-Germain.

Translated into English the plaque says:

In this building from 1910–1920 lived
Edith Wharton
American Writer
1862–1937
She was the first American writer to move to France
for the love of this country and of its literature.
'My years of Paris life were spent entirely in the rue de Varenne –
rich years, crowded and happy years.'
Like Henry James, the work of Edith
Wharton brought to life – in delicate and biting style –
the high society of which she was a part.
Association la Mémoire des Lieux

The French admire Edith Wharton because she was a great writer who lived in Paris. And they appreciate her because, unlike so many, she stayed in Paris during World War One. She worked tirelessly to assist impoverished refugees and campaigned to persuade the United States government to enter the war. The French gave Mrs Wharton a Legion of Honor and even today regard her as something of a national monument.

Edith Wharton actually looked a bit like a monument, rather large and solid. Her jaw-line was square enough to serve as a plinth. The patrician's aristocrat, Edith actively encouraged strangers to feel intimidated by her. After all, her aunt was the exclusive Mrs Jones of New York, whose relocation to a house further up 5th Avenue gave rise to the term *keeping up with the Joneses.*

Even her best friend, Henry James, was a little frightened of Mrs Wharton, and referred to her variously as The Angel of Devastation, Bonaparte and Attila. On the rare occasions when he was persuaded to visit Edith Wharton, Henry James felt like a captive prisoner. From the luxury of rue de Varenne he wrote to a friend: *I am kept here in golden chains, in gorgeous bondage, in breathless attendance and beautiful asservissement.*

I suspect it suited Edith Wharton to retain some distance in most of her relationships. She wasn't a confessional type: she liked to keep her own counsel. In society she approved of stimulating general conversation, not personal revelation. And she was particularly careful to keep strangers and hangers-on at a distance. Mrs Wharton is never more aloof than in this truly pompous segment of her autobiography, *A Backward Glance*:

> *Among the friendships then made I should like to record with particular gratitude that of the Countess Papafava of Padua, from whom I first heard of the fantastic Castel of Cattajo, and through whose kindness the intricately lovely gardens of Val San Zibio were opened to me; of Don Guildo Cagnola of Varese, an authority on Italian villa architecture, and himself the owner of La Gazzada, the beautiful villa near Varese of which there is a painting by Canaletto in the Brera; of the countess Rasponi, who lived in the noble villa of . . .*

And so, I regret to advise, Edith Wharton continues on for some paragraphs. Much of *A Backward Glance* is like this, and, as a tactic to distance the presumptuous reader, it works superbly.

Edith Wharton, the formidable hostess, the magisterial author, the patrician American – these personae were real. But there was more to Edith Wharton than this.

From the outside Edith Wharton's former home is austere and severe, surrounded by embassies and other grand homes. But as I peer into the privacy of her court-yard, I can see a burst of wisteria – delicate, mauve, playful – springing up the sandy walls and tumbling over the black wrought-iron balconies.

⚜

Now meet another Edith Wharton, a woman unravelled by passion. *She felt like a slave, and a goddess, and a girl in her teens . . .*

In June 1909, at the age of forty-seven, Edith Wharton consummated a romance with a journalist named Morton Fullerton. He was the grand folly of her life; the one man for whom she sacrificed all pride, all dignity, all *hauteur.* She had always kept a daily diary; now she kept a separate love diary in which she addressed Fullerton as *you,* recorded all their moments together and traced the hopeful surges and timid retreats of her emotions.

Morton Fullerton was a complex man, a character who might, in fact, have been found in a novel by either Henry James or Edith Wharton. He was bisexual. He was also itinerant, decadent, charming and unreliable. His nature made it impossible for him to live in the bright sunlight of his American homeland; he was better suited to the more forgiving shadows and corners of European capitals. Even while he was conducting his affair with Edith Wharton, Fullerton was managing several other compli-cated relationships.

In *The Age of Innocence* and *The House of Mirth*, Mrs

Wharton has mastery of a chaotic universe. She is sane, compassionate, satirical. Who would have thought a love affair with a second-rate journalist would undo this great author? Yet it does. She is reduced to the same embarrassing clichés used by every woman in love. She writes terrible poetry in honor of their sexual encounters. She is grateful, anxious, tremulous.

Here she is worrying about clothes: *There is the black dress I had on the first time we went to the Sorbonne to hear B[aker] lecture last December. I remember thinking: Will he like me in it? . . . There is the tea-gown I wore the first night you dined with me alone . . . You liked it, you said . . .*

Here she is, amazed that wonderful *he* could love unworthy *her: I don't suppose you know, since it is more of my sex than yours – the quiet ecstasy I feel sitting next to you in a public place, looking now and then at the way the hair grows on your forehead, at the line of your profile turned to the stage, your attitude, your expression – while every drop of blood in my body whispers: 'Mine-mine-mine'.*

Of course, Fullerton wasn't hers, hers, hers at all, and the relationship eventually fizzled out in a sad flurry of pleading letters from Edith. But I don't think we need to pity Edith Wharton her painful love affair. It was one of the great experiences of her life. Worse than too much pain was the prospect of no sensation at all. Edith once wrote a searing image of a life lived without deep experiences, a life untouched:

I have sometimes thought that a woman's nature is like a great house full of rooms: there is the hall, through which everyone passes going in and out; the drawing room, where one receives formal visits; the sitting room, where members of the family come and go as they list; but beyond that, far beyond, are other rooms, the handles of

*whose doors are never turned, no one knows the way to them, no
one knows whither they lead; and in the innermost room, the holy
of holies, the soul sits alone and waits for a footstep that never
comes.*

This, in fact, expresses Edith's view of the kind of life
she felt condemned to live in America – a life of surface
activity but deep inner loneliness. Edith was in her late
forties when she began her affair with Morton Fullerton.
She was at her peak as a writer and a woman. She wanted
to open all the doors of her soul, no matter how invasive
the visitor might be.

⚜

In Edith's expansion as a woman, Paris was important.
America, she felt, condemned a woman to live within a
category: *I was a failure in Boston . . . because they thought
I was too fashionable to be intelligent, and a failure in New York
because they were afraid I was too intelligent to be fashionable.*
In Paris, however, there was space for Edith Wharton to be
fully herself, to explore the heights and depths of her own
character.

Moreover, unlike the Americans, the French understood pleasure, and its importance. *It is only in sophisticated
societies that intellectuals recognize the uses of the frivolous,* she
said. Edith Wharton wanted to be fashionable and frivolous and sophisticated and intelligent all at the same time.
She wanted the precious right to be contradictory. Why
shouldn't she transcend the tedium of strict categories for
women and their behavior? She realized she couldn't be
various, spicy and contradictory in America. It was a
society that dealt in simplicities. But in Paris, well, it was
quite different.

After her death, when the first biographies of Edith Wharton were being written, Morton Fullerton wanted people to understand the extent to which Mrs Wharton had achieved complexity and completeness. *Please seize the event*, he urged, *however delicate the problem, to dispel the myth of your heroine's frigidity . . .*

✤

It's a solitary figure I make, a thirty-something woman with her bright lipstick and her black leather bag strapped across her shoulder. I'm conscious of my aloneness as I walk through the quiet streets of the Faubourg Saint-Germain and listen to my footsteps rebound off the pavement. No one is waiting for me; no obligations require my attention. I am surplus to social requirements. Perhaps I should feel lonely. But I don't. Like a cat, I choose to be pleased with myself and my own company. I prowl these ancient streets with a sly sense of freedom.

Dispel the myth of your heroine's frigidity, urged Morton Fullerton. But frigidity was a myth that clung long and hard to Edith Wharton. Janet Flanner, the *New Yorker's* acerbic Paris correspondent, referred to her after her death as the *literary, correct, meticulous Mrs Wharton . . .* She went on, acidly: *From the Rue de Varenne* [Edith Wharton] *finally started her frigid conquest of the faubourg . . . Mrs Wharton was perhaps too formal even for the faubourg.*

There's a reason why Janet Flanner was so harsh on Edith Wharton. Flanner was a prominent member of the artistic community in Paris which gathered around the charismatic and revolutionary figure of Gertrude Stein. Mrs Wharton must have seemed quite the stuffy Grande Dame with her *belle époque* gowns and her Proustian salons compared to the breakthrough salon hosted by Miss Stein at rue de Fleurus.

What Janet Flanner didn't, perhaps, understand was just how much Edith Wharton and Gertrude Stein had in common. These two women couldn't have been more different, yet they shared a set of ideas about Paris, about tradition and freedom, about the role of a civilized society and the place of women in it.

In 1940, Gertrude Stein published a book called *Paris, France*. It is a love letter to her adopted country. It opens with, and then intermittently repeats, this curious little refrain: *Paris, France is exciting and peaceful.* At first I hated this phrase. How could somewhere be both exciting *and* peaceful? The phrase lacked all logic, even poetic logic. It seemed to me sloppy writing of the worst and most pretentious kind. And at first I found the book itself hard going (what grudge did Ms Stein have against punctuation?).

But this funny little book gradually drew me in. Ms Stein proceeds by degrees to explore why a fundamentally conservative society provided the fertile soil for breakthrough modernism. Through her portraits of bourgeois servants and peasants and shopkeepers and pets she reveals a society based on tradition, order and ritual. She shows us something of the worldly, unsparing French acceptance of human nature and life and death. France, according to Ms Stein, is a complex, unsentimental, deeply civilized society. She says: *The French need to be civilized and in order to do so . . . must have tradition and freedom.* Tradition and freedom.

Twenty years earlier, in 1919, Edith Wharton wrote her own love letter to France, *French Ways and their Meaning.* Of course, Mrs Wharton's world is sprinkled rather more with dukes and *Académiciens*. But, from her very different perspective, she arrives at a similar conclusion.

Mrs Wharton said:

There is a reflex of negation, of rejection, at the very root of the French character: an instinctive recoil from the new, the untasted, the untested, like the retracting of an insect's feelers at contact with an unfamiliar object; and no one can hope to understand the French without bearing in mind that this unquestioning respect for rules of which the meaning is forgotten acts as a perpetual necessary check to the idol-breaking instinct of the freest minds in the world. It may sound like a poor paradox to say that the French are traditional about small things because they are so free about big ones.

Like the decisive clues in the treasure hunt, up pop those twin ideas again: *tradition* and *freedom*. For these two very different women, Paris, traditional and free, created a kind of creative space. A space within which to invent an art, or a life.

It was easy to tag Edith Wharton as an old fuddy-duddy. It's well known that she didn't admire James Joyce or TS Eliot. Nor did she enjoy Radclyffe Hall's controversial lesbian novel *The Well of Loneliness*. But her objections were aesthetic, not moral. The form of things was very important to her. How you did, artistically speaking, was every bit as important as what you did. And indeed, the traditional nineteenth-century forms and style of Mrs Wharton's novels have to some extent overshadowed the genuinely progressive ideas within them.

In fact, Mrs Wharton, traditional on the outside, was wonderfully free on the inside. She relished the flowing dance of Isadora Duncan. *It shed light on every kind of beauty*, she thought. Diaghilev, with composer Stravinsky and his Ballet Russes, *broke down old barriers of convention*, she said, with his *wild, free measures*. She was an admirer of the groundbreaking *Le Sacre du Printemps* and *L'Oiseau de Feu*.

And then there's Gertrude Stein. She is credited with the birth of modernism in her salon. She was a lesbian, an iconoclast, a revolutionary user of language. Her friends included the literary and artistic avant-garde, like Hemingway and Picasso. Yet this wasn't the whole story either. Underneath the revolutionary veneer, Gertrude and Alice lived with the order and regularity of the most stolid bourgeois couple. They were as tidy and fussy as maiden aunts, except that instead of pastel landscapes, they had modernist masterpieces on their walls.

In the end then, Edith Wharton and Gertrude Stein – and who would wish to downplay how wonderfully different they were? – created an orderly framework for their extraordinary lives. Mrs Wharton's rather secretive progressiveness co-existed comfortably with a deep respect for tradition and old gardens and refined manners. Equally, Gertrude Stein's radicalism co-existed comfortably with dry teas and walking the dogs. Tradition and freedom they sought, and won.

But there's more.

Paris was important both to Edith Wharton and Gertrude Stein because of the way it treated women. In Paris, women were not deemed additional or ornamental to civilization: they were the instrument and the evidence of civilization. Women *were* civilization.

The more civilized a society is, the wider is the range of each woman's influence over men, and of each man's influence over women, said Edith Wharton. *Intelligent and cultivated people of either sex will never limit themselves to communing within their own households . . . The long hypocrisy which Puritan England handed on to America concerning the danger of frank and free social relations between men and women has done more than anything else to retard real civilisation in America.*

Gertrude Stein echoed this view: *The relation of men to women and men to men and women to women in a state of being civilized has very much to be considered. Frenchmen love older women, that is women who have already done more living, and that has something to do with civilisation.*

Of all the things Gertrude Stein said about Paris, her most famous line is this: *It's not what Paris gave you but what it didn't take away from you that was important.*

I think what Paris didn't take away from Gertrude, or Edith, or the dozens of other women who came here, was their invented selves, their created womanhood. In Paris they could be the kind of women they chose to be, straight or gay, promiscuous or monogamous, creative, independent, open, traditional and free.

That's why Paris was exciting. And that's why it was peaceful too.

⚜

In Australia we do girls very well: young, fresh, ignorant, sexy girls. Not that I was one of them. I was pale and bookish and wore black tights in winter and secondhand sixties' frocks in summer. It's not as though I didn't try to become a sun-burnished bikini type, but it simply didn't work. I certainly didn't catch the boys: all I got was a sunburn.

In France they like women, grown-up women. Ellen once said to me that the French don't consider that a woman starts to become interesting until she is thirty-five years old. It's why Paris always attracted older women of fame or substance, like Maria Callas or Olivia de Havilland or Pamela Harriman, who felt appreciated here. (And why so few French women emigrate. When Germaine de Staël went to England she was genuinely puzzled by the way English women were treated. *'Is a woman a minor forever in your country?'* she asked her neighbor Susannah Phillips. *'It seems to me that your sister* [novelist Fanny Burney] *is like a girl of fourteen.'*)

But what does it mean to be a woman, a grown-up woman? When you're young you imagine that maturity of mind must, automatically, accompany a maturing body. Except it doesn't happen. You can get to thirty-five and still feel like a little child.

The truth is, we aren't psychologically rewarded for adulthood anymore and all our advertising is directed to how we can stay *young* and *fresh* and *carefree*. It used to be that children were solemnly initiated into adulthood. Menstruation, a twenty-first birthday, or marriage, or the birth of a child – these were the milestones. And causes for ritual celebration. But not anymore. Or at least, not as demonstrations of adulthood.

Even as a schoolgirl laboring up the hill to the white convent, I knew I wanted to grow up. I wanted to be a worldly woman, although I hardly knew what that meant. And I sensed that it would be hard to achieve this in Australia, an ancient continent but a young country, a teenage nation. In the end, of course, my solution was to seek out exotic travel and interesting jobs and look for the great conversations that would shape the clueless teenager into a sophisticated woman. I'm not sure I had much success.

Years ago, when I was on my first and only diplomatic posting to Belgrade, the senior local staff member was a plump Serbian aristocrat named Marina. She had been part of the Embassy for twenty years. 'Darling,' she said to me, with her ruined smile, 'I have seen so many of you

Australian women. You are all the same. You are romantics.'
She said this as if it were a dirty word. 'You expect too
much,' she said. 'You're always disappointed. You expect
the men to be something they are not. Darling,' she said,
'you have to learn how to manage men. European
women,' she repeated smugly, spreading her moist ringed
hands, 'we know how to manage men.'

I hung my head for a moment, and then returned to my
dark little office and resumed hand-wringing and heartbreaking over my faraway boyfriend's infidelities. I knew
she was right, but what could I do?

Edith Wharton thought about this issue too and, with
some rare compassion towards her countrywomen,
concluded that American women couldn't help but be
immature simply *because* they were American.

Why does the European woman interest herself so much more in
what the men are doing? Because she's so important to them that
they make it worth her while! She's not a parenthesis, as she is
here – she's in the very middle of the picture. Where does the real
life of most American men lie? In some woman's drawing room or
in their offices? The answer's obvious isn't it. The emotional center
of gravity's not the same in the two hemispheres. In the effete soci-
eties it's love, in our new one it's business.

Gertrude Stein also carefully calibrated levels of
national maturity. She too concluded that the character
of a nation had a very real effect on the lives and disposi-
tion of its citizens.

France really prefers civilisation to tumultuous adolescence, France
prefers that the adolescent learns reserve and logic and civilisation
and fashion as he emerges out of adolescence, France who thinks that

childhood and adolescence should be felt instinctively as not an end in itself but as a progression toward the state of being civilised.

Once again, you see, there's that link between civilization and art and being grown-up.

Here's Edith Wharton again: *No nation can have grown-up ideas till it has a ruling caste of grown-up men and women; and it is possible to have a ruling caste of grown-up men and women only in a civilization where the power of each sex is balanced by that of the other.*

So now we come to a distinctly infuriating Catch 22. To get a grown-up society you need grown-up women. But you can't mould and form grown-up women, except in a grown-up society.

Some people think it's grown-up for women of a certain age to put sex behind them. They think that sex is a pastime of youth and immaturity. But the French don't. They don't equate sex with age. They equate sex with sexiness.

Sexuality is a very personal thing, of course. But I don't see why a woman should have to declare herself sexually washed up at some arbitrary age, any more than she would declare herself intellectually completed. Sexuality is not like a small-town festival that the deputy mayor dutifully declares to be closed, or an inner light that a resentful warden suddenly switches off. Part of the trick, though, is finding in yourself a certain adult sexuality, which is, I think, a different quality from youthful sexuality. It's more subtle, like old wine or antique jewelry.

Of course, the women of Paris offer sure evidence of the potential appeal of the older woman. Here's a list I made up – it's a roll-call of grown-up sexiness: Edith Wharton had her love affair with Morton Fullerton when she was forty-seven. George Sand was sixty years old when she took her last lover, Charles Marchal. He was thirty-six. She wrote: *It is as if I see everything for the first time.* Germaine de Staël made her second marriage at the age of forty-five. Her husband was twenty-three years old. Nancy Mitford commenced her great love affair with Gaston Palewski when she was in her early forties.

Then there was Colette, who serves as proof that being a grown-up woman doesn't make you good, necessarily, or wise. But it sure does make you sexy. In 1920, Colette was forty-seven years old. She was a very powerful, sexual woman. But even today it still seems shocking that she began a discreet affair with her sixteen-year-old stepson, Bertrand de Jouvenal.

It was summer and the young, handsome and earnest Bertrand was staying with his stepmother and two of her younger girlfriends at his father's holiday house in Brittany. Colette's novel *Chéri*, about the doomed love affair between an ageing courtesan and a young gigolo, was being serialized in the newspaper. No wonder, then, that Bertrand noticed Colette looking at him one day as he ran in off the beach. When she passed her arm around his waist he trembled. She kissed him goodnight – on the mouth.

Soon after that the three women decided it was time to make a man of this beautiful boy. Colette suggested to Bertrand that his sexual initiation take place with the youngest of the three women, Germaine Beaumont. But by then, Bertrand had succumbed to Colette emotionally. Bertrand told a friend that his stepmother had been *demanding, voracious, expert and rewarding.* Their liaison lasted, on and off, for nearly five years.

Here's another story about wilfulness and sexiness. During World War Two Coco Chanel stayed on in the Hôtel Ritz, which had been commandeered by the German High Command. She formed a relationship with Baron Hans Gunther von Dinklage, a Nazi. He was one of those urbane German aristocrats who wangled a tour in Paris and treated the Nazi regime and the war as a rather tiresome but necessary irritant. At the end of the war Chanel was interrogated. When asked if it were true that she had consorted with a German, she reportedly replied: *'Really, a woman of my age cannot be expected to look at his passport if she has a chance of a lover.'*

Of course, at fifty-seven, Coco Chanel was more beautiful than ever. And women like Josephine and Nancy Mitford took great care about their appearance into their later years. But George Sand, according to Charles Dickens, was as plain as Queen Victoria's nurse. Edith Wharton was immaculately dressed but looked like a bad statue in a public park. And Germaine de Staël was overweight and tastelessly dressed.

You see, it was never about how they looked, it was about their vitality and verve and spirit. They had worked it out: how to be, as a woman, as an older woman. And they didn't deny themselves their own sexuality.

⚜

It's one of those bright and calm Sundays which are worthy of your Sunday best. As I walk from Rachel's to Omar's restaurant, I savor the slower pace of the *quartier*, the gentler tone. At Chez Omar I tentatively push open the heavy restaurant door. In the gloom I see several young men sitting and leaning and smoking. They seem neither surprised nor interested to see me. From the placid

Parisian sidewalk I feel as though I have accidentally walked in on an out-take from a mob movie.

One of the young men walks out the back. Omar emerges, dapper and unconcerned. We step outside, and after a moment the young man pulls up in a large Mercedes. Omar takes over the driving and I am ushered gently but impersonally into the passenger seat.

Omar takes me to lunch at the Dôme restaurant, one of the famous old brasseries of Montparnasse. He tells me that when he arrived in Paris as a young migrant from North Africa he used to work here as a waiter, and later at nearby La Coupole. But now he is an important man, and the waiters treat him with elaborate and practiced deference. We take our seats and eat fine, bland sole. I have a glass of wine: Omar doesn't drink. It's all rather like being taken out for a treat by your great-uncle.

Omar seems, well, not particularly interested in me. He doesn't ask me a lot of questions. He seems content merely to sit and chat intermittently, in a rather desultory fashion. I try to coax some memories of his earlier days in Paris, but I can see it's all a bit hazy now. Or perhaps not important. I realize that this is a quiet man, a peaceful man. He has made his money, he is looking after his extended family, he is respected and admired.

Every now and then Omar surprises me with an observation.

'At La Coupole you know,' he says, 'there is a dance hall downstairs.'

'Oh?' I say.

'Older women would come there to dance with the young men,' he goes on, 'to find comfort.'

'Really?' I say.

But the conversation goes no further.

Our puzzling discourse unsettles me and suddenly ignites memories of my younger self. For a long time I had only the most tenuous hold on my identity. Friends and family would treat me as if I was a known personality with distinctive characteristics. But deep inside I felt unformed. I looked at the world from behind a regulation set of eyes, but inside my skin I was little more than a mass of emotions and sensations. As the French say, I didn't feel *bien dans ma peau*. I simply did not know how to bring my floating attributes together into a coherent personality. And so I sometimes found it hard to connect with people, to discover the self beneath their skins. I guess I was simply a young woman, and a late developer. I guess I am still developing.

After lunch Omar seems to brighten up. 'Now I shall show you a little bit of Paris,' he says. 'Shall we go to La Mosquée?'

La Mosquée is beautiful. It sits on the edge of the 5th *arrondissement* near the Jardin des Plantes. Under the white minaret it's a 1920s Moorish-style complex with white colonnades, tinkling fountains and blue-green tiled courtyards. There's the mosque itself, a library and a bathhouse. And a *salon de thé*, elaborately decorated with banquettes and a painted ceiling and cushions and mosaics and rich colors. After we've had a look around, we adjourn to the little salon courtyard and eat sweets and drink mint tea from gold-patterned colored glasses. The Sunday light filters into the space.

For the first time, Omar appears at home, and I realize that this little part of Paris, this island of Islam, means more to him than all the flashy restaurants frequented by his own clientele. Here he seems complete as an Algerian and a Parisian. This sense of cultural melding reminds me of the gorgeous African women I see on the Métro, with their licorice curls and full lips. They accessorize their brightly colored cotton turbans and kaftans with stiletto heels. They add a joyous new dimension to traditional chic.

Once I might have felt a nervous compulsion to clown and patter and tease this curious gentleman taking me out for the afternoon. But now I relax with him into a Sunday mood. I simply sit and enjoy his stories of his family. Some of it I don't really understand — it's a conversation directed not at me, but at some interior space in his memory, or his heart.

Before we depart the conversation drifts to the tragic death in Paris of the English Princess Diana. Omar suddenly looks very serious.

'You know that Diana was killed because of her relationship with a Muslim man.'

I look startled.

'Sure, of course,' he says bitterly. 'She was free here. But the British, they couldn't let her be.'

We walk back to the car and Omar tentatively passes an arm around my waist. I gently drift out of his embrace. We smile cautiously.

As Omar drops me off he says to me, 'Come and see me next time you are in Paris.' And, 'Will you write about me and my restaurant?'

I walk through the door to see Rachel lying on her *chaise longue* reading *Vanity Fair*.

'How was that?' she asks.

'Odd,' I say. 'But good.'

⚜

Edith Wharton's death was a major public event. She was a great and famous author, very rich and well respected. And she had planned her death well. Her letters and papers were in order. She had even marked some documents clearly, *For my biographer*. She was well aware that history would judge her and that her letters and documents would eventually form part of a fuller picture of Mrs Wharton.

But no one was prepared for this. In her desk was a fragment of a novella and it was pornography. Superbly written and realized, but clearly, pornography. It reveals its author to be a woman with a detailed knowledge of sex and sensuality. A woman who has, as the French might say, been well and thoroughly fucked.

Here's just a little of what Mrs Wharton wrote:

As his hand stole higher she felt the secret bud of her body swelling, yearning, quivering hotly to burst into bloom. Ah, here was his subtle forefinger pressing it, forcing its tight petals softly apart, and laying on their sensitive edges a circular touch so soft and yet so fiery that already lightnings of heat shot from that palpitating center all over her surrendered body, to the tips of her fingers, and the ends of her loosened hair. The sensation was so exquisite that she could have asked to have it indefinitely prolonged; but suddenly his head bent lower, and with a deeper thrill she felt his lips pressed upon that quivering invisible bud, and then the delicate firm thrust of his tongue, so full and yet so infinitely subtle, pressing apart the close petals and forcing itself in deeper and deeper through the passage that glowed and seemed to become illuminated at its approach . . .

To add to the taboo-breaking frisson of this passage, I should tell you that it describes the first formal act of incest between a father and his adult daughter.

And it was written in 1935 when Edith Wharton was seventy-three years old.

⌁ 13 ⌁

But Women *Are* Politics . . .

What else is happiness but the development of our
abilities . . .?

Germaine de Staël

W<small>HEN</small> I <small>WORKED</small> in Canberra, I came across quite a
few women in politics. Labor women, mostly. They were
nearly all graduates of seventies' feminism, and many
had found their way to national politics via the trade
union movement. They had fought hard for the sister-
hood and were enjoying the spoils of victory. All padded
flesh and hefty heartiness, they would bustle in to see
the Deputy Prime Minister, as loud as their big-
shouldered suits. They would lecture him with
finger-wagging vigor on child-care and maternity leave.
The Deputy Prime Minister would laugh vaguely and

wave them away, promising, perhaps, to do something, sometime.

Yet despite the big hair and bright makeup, despite the correctly feminist issues and domineering maternal banter, I was always struck, in the end, by how similar these women politicians were to their male counterparts. Like the men, these women had somehow de-sexed themselves. That's not to say that politicians didn't have sex lives, far from it: Canberra is a notoriously lusty city. Rather, that all those men and women in public life had consciously put their intimate selves and their professional selves into separate compartments. The bedroom was kept a long, long way from the office.

As I stroll past the Palais Bourbon, home to the French Parliament, and into the creamy heart of the Faubourg Saint-Germain, every now and then I pass an exquisite shop displaying finely embroidered bed linen or filmy hand-stitched silk nightgowns. The French are completely at home in the bedroom: in fact, for centuries bedrooms played an important role in French public life. The Bourbon Kings conducted a formal *lever* and *coucher*, often held in a large, grand room away from their actual sleeping quarters. It was a great privilege for a courtier to attend the King's rising and retiring ceremonies. Moreover, whenever the King presided over parliamentary sessions, he did so on a canopied bed, the *lit de justice*. This was a curious but apparently potent symbol of the King's divine, supreme power. Some think that Louis XVI sealed his fate when he fell asleep on his *lit de justice*, snoring his way through a critical parliamentary debate in the early stages of the Revolution.

The French bedroom had an important social function as well. The seventeenth-century salon hostesses often received friends in their bedrooms. Many had little couches known as *ruelles* (little streets) built between their beds and the walls for their friends to lie upon while visiting. Bedrooms are still a source of uncomplicated fascination in France. I've been to see Marcel Proust's bedroom reconstructed in the Musée Carnavelet and Madame de Récamier's bedroom in the Louvre. The beds always seem remarkably small, as if an earlier France was populated by exquisite diminutives.

But right now there is only one French bedroom that really interests me. It belongs to a political activist who not only refused to be de-sexed by public life, but who openly smashed through the conventional demarcation lines between public life and private passion. She lived between the tumultuous years of 1766 and 1817 and her name was Germaine de Staël. She was, Lord Byron thought, *the first female writer of this, perhaps of any age.*

Germaine de Staël's bedroom was Europe's headquarters for liberal politics and progressive ideas. A succession of lovers – soldiers and statesmen, diplomats and scholars – owed their careers to her influence and inspiration. In between amorous exchanges she obtained their appointments and sinecures, she edited speeches and essays, she advised on tactics and policies, she clarified lines of thinking and corrected logical errors. None of which interfered in the least with her own enormous workload: writing essays and novels, hosting the most important salon in Europe and, finally, emerging as the leading dissident against Napoleon. All achieved without any official political appointment.

In the course of reading about the women of Paris, Germaine de Staël came as a major discovery to me. I felt quite shocked that I had never heard of her. I wanted to

say, well, I knew a bit about Napoleon and Wellington and
Talleyrand. So why wasn't I told about Germaine de Staël?
Hey?

In truth, Germaine de Staël's life story moves and
disturbs me. There could be many reasons for this. One
may be that her life raises the distinctly unsettling question
of women and power.

⚜

I'm at number 52 rue de Varenne and standing in front of
a plaque (again). There must be thousands of these plaques
pasted around Paris, like postcards from history. But this is
my favorite. Translated, it says:

> Hôtel de Galliffet: Cultural Institute of Italy
> Talleyrand made this the center of political life under the
> Directory as Minister for Foreign Affairs. It was here that
> Madame de Staël was presented to Napoleon Bonaparte on
> 3 January 1798, and the beginning of their mutual hostility.

Imagine a cold and beautiful winter's evening. The
biggest party since the *ancien régime* is underway. Stepping
from their carriages, five hundred guests stroll through this
courtyard where rows of classical white columns are
emblazoned with martial images: the vivid tents and
banners recall Napoleon's recent heroics in Italy. Inside the
lovely house the scent of amber lingers in the air, intensified by thousands of candles hung on low, glittering
chandeliers. Flowers line the staircases. For the first time in
France, the waltz is being played, and the thin dresses
balloon gently as the women sway and turn. Dazzled by
their own glamor, it gradually dawns upon the guests that
they are being elected into a new French political elite.

And this is just what their host Talleyrand is trying to achieve, because tonight he inaugurates a new kind of aristocracy. With a new kind of king.

From her home around the corner in the rue du Bac, Germaine de Staël arrives at the ball, a colorful figure with her bright turban and dark curls. She sweeps through the courtyard, impervious to the glitzy atmosphere. She's seen this kind of thing before. Her Swiss father was a banker, one of the richest men in France. He served for a time as Louis XVI's finance minister. Her host, Talleyrand, was her first lover, and he owes his appointment as foreign minister to her political influence. She knows only too well the strengths and weaknesses of this new breed of politician. After all, most of them attend her salon. As far as Germaine de Staël is concerned, this phase of the Revolution has merely *put the villains-for-the-love-of-profit in the place of the villains-for-the-love-of-crime.*

As the ball reaches its climax Talleyrand, with his famous limp, slowly leads in his guest of honor: it's Josephine, gently regal in a thin gown and a diadem of antique cameos. But Germaine's focus is upon the man following behind – uniformed, modest, sallow, short, heroic Napoleon. Like many moderates, she believes his combination of revolutionary passion and military know-how may offer France the best hope of stability and democracy.

So she waylays him at the bottom of the stairs. She turns up again in the small salon. She pursues him on the way to the table. She tries every one of her conversational gambits. She is one of the most influential people in France and she can *help* Napoleon. She wants Napoleon to respond to her, to engage with her, to *recognize* her, yes, perhaps even to fall under her famous spell. But he doesn't.

The final conversation goes so badly that people talk about it for years.

> *'General!' exclaims Madame de Staël. 'Who most represents your idea of a wife?'*
>
> *'Mine!' replies Napoleon. Germaine persists.*
>
> *'That is simple enough, but what kind of woman would you admire the most?'*
>
> *'She who is the best housekeeper,' answers the hero.*
>
> *Finally Germaine demands of him: 'Who is the greatest woman, alive or dead?'*
>
> *Bonaparte looks at her. 'The one who has made the most children,' he says.*

The plaque says that this was the beginning of their *mutual hostility* – the phrase binding these two great adversaries together: after all, only equals have *mutual* feelings.

But the truth is that the feeling wasn't, at first, mutual – it was only Napoleon who was hostile. And, really, I can understand why. It must have been infuriating to have the question of *woman* put to him so directly – it must have seemed like a full-frontal assault. From that moment, Napoleon viewed Germaine de Staël through the prism of her femininity: she had, effectively, demanded it. Until the day he died, Napoleon's epithets for Germaine de Staël never failed to allude to her gender: *That hussy Staël*, he called her. Or *that whore, and an ugly one at that*. Or *that mad woman*. Eventually she became just *that woman*.

Germaine de Staël, however, did not indulge in personal politics. In the absence of better leadership options for France, she set aside Napoleon's personal dislike. She continued to endorse him and engage with him. Once she even turned up at Napoleon's little house in rue Chantereine. Told by the butler that Napoleon was naked in his bath she cried, *No matter, genius has no sex!*

When Napoleon came back from Egypt and mounted a military coup against the Directory Government in November 1799, Germaine de Staël remained a reluctant supporter. But she had her limits. As Napoleon became more socially conservative, as he drifted towards totalitarianism and war-mongering, she pulled back. Pragmatic, yes, but she was never going to be an uncritical supporter of the emerging Napoleonic state.

On the evening of 4 January 1800, Germaine de Staël's lover Benjamin Constant was drafting his maiden speech to Napoleon's newly formed Tribunate. Benjamin Constant proposed to call for the Tribunate's independence and declare that otherwise *there would be nothing left but servitude and silence – a silence that all Europe would hear.* He knew this would provoke Napoleon's wrath. The same night there was a big gathering at Germaine de Staël's house. Half of Napoleon's cabinet and even several of his brothers were among the guests. Benjamin Constant warned Germaine, *'Tonight your drawing room is filled with people whom you like. If I make my speech it will be deserted tomorrow.'* Germaine de Staël told her lover simply, *'One must follow one's convictions.'*

Events transpired as Benjamin predicted. Napoleon was angry at the speech and blamed not Benjamin Constant, but his mistress, Germaine de Staël. Her regular guests suddenly avoided her salon. For a period she was socially ostracized. The press was already falling under Napoleon's control and attacked Germaine de Staël: *It is not your fault that you are ugly, but it is your fault that you are an intriguer.*

Towards the spring of 1800, Germaine de Staël published *On Literature*. The topic was literature, but the theme was artistic freedom.

Its success meant that I was back in society's favor. My salon was crowded with people again, and I rediscovered the pleasure of talking – talking in Paris – which I must admit has always been the most stimulating pleasure I have ever known. My book said not one word about Bonaparte, but it did contain some very liberal sentiments, rather forcefully expressed.

More than anyone else, except perhaps Germaine herself, Napoleon recognized the significant subversive power of Germaine de Staël's 'liberal sentiments'. She was developing a coherent body of thought which challenged the dictatorial basis of his regime. He had his spies reporting her every conversation to him, receiving their reports as he sat in his bathtub. *I can smell her a mile away*, he steamed. At last he decided to neutralize this problematic political opponent. He asked his brother Joseph to find out what Madame de Staël wanted – *to stay in Paris? The restoration of funds owed by the French State to her father? What?* He should have known better.

'*It's not a question of what I want*,' said Germaine de Staël, '*but of what I think.*'

Napoleon and Germaine de Staël came face to face for the last time in early 1801. She had prepared any number of things to say to the First Consul. But Napoleon merely looked at her low-cut gown and exposed bosom and said brutally, '*You must have nursed all your children yourself, Madame?*'

Of course I wondered: well, what did Madame de Staël say in response? Did she snap back a witty one-liner? Take the humiliation and smile blankly? Flare up in anger? But history, in its infuriating way, does not record what happened next. I am sure, however, that I know how Germaine de Staël felt. She was a sensitive and reflective person. She felt the wound alright. It hurt. And there was worse to come.

In 1802, Napoleon made himself Consul for life. Having consolidated his position he now turned openly to menace. He said to his brother Joseph, *'Serve notice to that woman . . . Advise her not to block my path, no matter what it is, no matter where I choose to go. Or else, I shall break her, I shall crush her.'*

⚜

Germaine de Staël once declared something remarkable. *True pleasure for me*, she wrote, *can be found only in love, in Paris or in power.* Love and Paris, yes, how easy to nod in sympathetic recognition. But how many of us would regard power as a pleasure? How many would admit to it? Power has become a dirty word in modern life and hunger for political power is especially despised. And it was not as if Germaine de Staël had anything to gain by her political activism – in fact, as an enormously wealthy woman she had much to lose.

In the winter of 1802, Germaine de Staël published her first novel, *Delphine.* Set in revolutionary France, it was all about society's hypocrisy and cruelty to an ardent and gifted woman. It was an instant bestseller. Even the English tourists in Paris stayed in their hotel rooms, sharing the novel around until each had completed it. *We are all in floods of tears*, Lady Bessborough wrote home to London.

But this was a very interesting document. It was politics disguised as literature. *Delphine* promoted the rights of women at a time when Napoleon was suppressing their independence; it implicitly criticized the Catholic Church just when Napoleon was negotiating the Concordat with the Pope; and it generally praised freedom of conscience when Napoleon was exerting complete State control. To add to the insult, his name was not mentioned once.

Napoleon was inflamed with rage by *Delphine*. For one intoxicating moment he thought about murdering Germaine de Staël. But he came up with an alternative, one which seemed to Germaine de Staël to be almost as cruel. Napoleon expelled her from France: the exile would last twelve long years. Germaine de Staël said bleakly, *The universe is in France; outside it, there is nothing.*

⚜

This is the rue du Bac. During her years of exile, whenever she thought of Paris, Germaine de Staël's thoughts flew to this street. She had opened her first salon here in 1786, as the twenty-year-old bride of the Swedish Ambassador. Of course, I tried to discover exactly which house she lived in, but accounts conflict. Perhaps this is it, perhaps this elegant townhouse at number 102 was where the young salonnière welcomed her guests? I'm not sure. I do know that Germaine de Staël resided in various houses around this area: the 7th *arrondissement* was her special patch of Paris. This street was important because it symbolized all that Germaine de Staël loved about the city, and all that she was forced to leave behind.

Germaine de Staël found no consolation in the fact that her exile was spent in palatial luxury at her grand estate, Coppet, outside Geneva. She called Switzerland a *magnificent horror* and railed against *the infernal peace* of Coppet. The company of her provincial neighbors only exacerbated her despair: *Please consider that, since my child-hood, I have lived with the most distinguished and noble subjects; then ask yourself what it costs me to hear discussed from morning till evening whether Miss So-and-So, who bores me, will marry Mr So-and-So, who produces the same effect on me.* England offered no alternative: *I turn this country over in every direction to see it as something other than a panorama, and so far I have been unsuccessful . . . What I feel above all is boredom. Ah, the gutter of the rue du Bac!* she would sigh.

Sometimes Germaine de Staël would sneak back into France; a few times she even made it all the way into Paris. Heavily disguised, she would take nightly walks, breathing the treasured air of the 7th *arrondissement*. But Napoleon's spies were everywhere, and each time she was rounded up and sent packing once again.

For Germaine de Staël, France represented civilization – and to her, civilization meant love, politics, art and, most of all, conversation. *Conversation as talent*, she wrote, *exists only in France . . . In other countries, conversation provides politeness, discussion and friendship. In France it is an art . . .* She added, *German women rarely show the quick spirit which makes conversation live and ideas move. This kind of pleasure can only be found in the wittiest, most piquant Parisian society. You need the elite of a French capital for such rare entertainment.*

And the pleasure, the *rare entertainment*, was not empty or frivolous. When history's most formidable politician, Talleyrand, returned from exile in America towards the end of the Revolution, he limped straight to Madame de Staël's salon. Asked why he spent so much time with women instead of discussing politics, he replied, *But women* are *politics.* The pleasures that Germaine de Staël found in love, and Paris, and power, were, in a way, all part of the same project. The root word of politics is *polis*, the

Greek word for city. Paris, to Germaine de Staël, was the center of civilization. To be political, in her world view, was to be civilized. And that was a pleasure.

Today, this area remains one of the prettiest of the city, with its hidden gardens and fountains, antique shops and art galleries, rare-book sellers and interesting buildings. At one point rue du Bac narrows and becomes a cozy village with a little cluster of food shops. Perhaps it looked somewhat like this in Germaine de Staël's day. My eyes roam the serene eighteenth-century architecture with pleasure – fine pediments, wrought-iron balconies, moulded archways. Here's an elaborate Art Nouveau shopfront which, amid so much classical simplicity, seems astonishingly modern.

It seems to me now, thinking about Germaine de Staël, that she was trying to steer her way through – more than this, to manage – one of history's great transitions. She was probably the only person ever to have conversed on sympathetic terms both with Voltaire, grand old man of the Enlightened classical age, and Lord Byron, *enfant terrible* of the new Romantic era. Though she witnessed the abrupt demise of the old eighteenth-century order with its aristocrats and salons, witty women and enlightened philosophers, she did not overly mourn its passing. She was one of the few who took the glorious ideas behind the Age of Reason to their logical conclusion. She welcomed democracy. She rejoiced in the new aspirations towards liberty and equality. She wanted to be part of the new era, shaping it.

But it seemed that Madame du Deffand's rigorous defence of the old aristocratic system had not been without some justification. Successive Revolutionary administrations did not want to make room for accomplished women. Napoleon actively tried to suppress them. Germaine de Staël understood the problem better than anyone. She wrote:

> *Women annoyed Napoleon as rebels; they were of no use to his political desires on the one hand, and were less accessible than men to the hopes and fears dispensed by power on the other. As a result, he took pleasure in saying hurtful and vulgar things to women . . . From his early habits of Revolutionary days he also retained a certain Jacobin antipathy to brilliant Paris society, which was greatly influenced by women; he was afraid of the art of teasing which we must admit is characteristic of Frenchwomen. If Bonaparte had been willing to keep to the proud role of great general and first magistrate of the Republic, he would have floated with the height of genius above all the little stinging barbs of salon wit. Once he decided to become a parvenu king, however, the bourgeois gentleman on the throne, he was exposing himself to the kind of society satire which can only be repressed by the use of espionage and terror; and that is how, in fact, he repressed it.*

I have read a number of biographies of Napoleon, or double biographies of Napoleon and Josephine, and no comment on his psyche or his politics has struck me as so thoughtful, penetrating and plausible as this analysis by the woman he most disliked.

⚜

I take a seat in a very modest café, remarkable only for its display of dozens of brands of cigarettes, and I take out Germaine de Staël's second novel *Corinne or Italy*, published in 1807, during her period of exile. The novel concerns a half-Italian, half-English woman of genius and her relationship with a disenchanted Scottish Lord,

Oswald Nevile. They commence a passionate love affair, but each has a secret and it tears the relationship apart. Lord Nevile ends up marrying Corinne's half-sister, a woman of worth who lacks Corinne's sublime genius. He is stricken with guilt and grief at leaving Corinne and his marriage suffers. Her heart broken by the rupture with Lord Nevile, Corinne slowly dies, but not before reuniting the married couple and ensuring that their future relationship will always be bound to her memory.

Corinne or Italy is a flawed novel, but an astonishing work. Corinne is Germaine de Staël's alter-ego. She has the same black turbaned hair, moulded arms, dark, expressive eyes and gift of magical eloquence. Indeed, to emphasize the close relationship between herself and her subject, Germaine de Staël had her portrait painted as Corinne, complete with lyre and Neapolitan background.

From the beginning of the novel Germaine de Staël makes one thing clear: Corinne is uniquely superior. The first time we meet the celebrated lyric poet, she is about to be crowned festively at the Capitol in Rome:

> *Corinne sat in the chariot built in the ancient style, and white-clad girls walked alongside. Wherever she passed, perfumes were lavishly flung into the air. Everyone came forward to see her from their windows which were decorated with potted plants and scarlet hanging. Everyone shouted: Long Live Corinne! Long live genius! Long live beauty!*

At the festival in her honor, Corinne's gifts are extensively enumerated – her imagination, her artistic gifts, her intellectual brilliance, her profound virtue. Lord Nevile is openly amazed by her superiority. *'Astonishing person, who are you?'*

said Oswald. 'Where did you get so many charms that would seem to be mutually exclusive – sensitivity, depth, gaiety, grace, spontaneity, modesty? Are you an illusion? Do you mean unearthly happiness for the whole life of the one who encounters you?'

Even today, such a congratulatory self-portrait by a woman would be received with raised eyebrows. It's a shock to encounter Germaine de Staël's extravagant endorsement of herself. It's uncomfortable and exciting.

But there's something very strange about this book. Contemporaries were aware that Germaine de Staël was no Corinne. Corinne is portrayed as graceful and poised: Germaine was clumsy and gauche. As a young girl she famously fell out of her carriage and tripped over her gown as she was presented to King Louis XVI and Queen Marie Antoinette. Corinne is slender and elegant: President George Washington's envoy to France, Gouverneur Morris, adored Germaine de Staël but thought she looked like a chambermaid. Corinne is socially refined: the terribly British Duke of Marlborough, confronted at a London dinner party by Germaine de Staël with her embarrassingly low-cut gowns and incessant talk, cried: *'Let me out!'*

Most notable of all, where Corinne is pious, pure and romantically faithful, Germaine de Staël had many love affairs, most of them complex and tormented. Germaine de Staël's relationship with Benjamin Constant, for example, began in 1794 and more or less continued until about 1810. In the early months and years, Constant was as passionately captivated as any of Germaine de Staël's admirers: *In a word, she is a being apart, a superior being, such as appears but once in a century,* he raved.

But like all the others, Constant eventually chafed at the complex emotional binds with which Germaine de Staël held him captive: *Pursued by her incessant reproaches, always in the public view because of Germaine's situation, and never holding the tiller of my own life,* he lamented. He took to visiting brothels and writing compulsively about himself and Germaine in his diary. *It is a terrible relationship,* he wrote. *A man who no longer loves and a woman who does not want to stop being loved.* Each took other lovers – Benjamin even married another woman in secret – but he still felt tied to Germaine de Staël and was desperately unhappy about it.

Finally Benjamin Constant purged the experience by writing a novel, *Adolphe,* about an affair between a clinging older woman and a confused young man. One spring night in Paris in 1816, Constant read *Adolphe* to a spellbound audience of fifteen people. It took more than three hours. A stunned listener noticed that towards the end of the reading Constant began to shudder and sob. The audience, infected by this emotion, began to rock and groan. It was an atmosphere of great intensity. All of a sudden Constant's sobs took on a different quality: it became apparent that he was laughing hysterically. In his diary for that day Benjamin recorded, *Read my novel. Hysterics.*

When Benjamin writes despairingly of being *in the public view* as a result of his relationship with Germaine de Staël, he was not exaggerating. Here was no secluded artist. She was not at all like, say, Jane Austen, her exact contemporary, who was at that time leading a quiet life in the English provinces. Far from it. By the time she had finished writing the novel, Germaine de Staël was the premier political activist in Europe. From her base at Coppet, she was traversing the continent to confer with the Russian Tsar, British prime ministers and German philosophers. She published important political books and essays. When she was at home, her salon was the magnet for the growing European movement against Napoleon. Four years after the publication of *Corinne or Italy* a quip went around that there were three great powers in Europe – England, Russia and Madame de Staël. Later Napoleon would say, *Her house at Coppet became a veritable arsenal against me. One went there to win one's spurs.*

So when Germaine de Staël wrote and published *Corinne or Italy*, there was a lot more at stake than an artist's idealized self-portrait. Its author knew that her work would be closely examined by kings and queens, prime ministers and generals, political allies and enemies. And perhaps even Napoleon himself.

I'm not sure what Germaine de Staël had in mind when she wrote *Corinne or Italy*. She was a complex woman and this is a multi-layered work. Perhaps it is Germaine de Staël's lament for the ideal self that she never achieved. Perhaps it is her way of revealing what she regards as the inner, the true Germaine de Staël. Or perhaps this is a very clever work of education. Corinne is intensely feminine. Unlike her extravagant and controversial creator, she is everything a woman of her times ought to have been. Yet even this paragon demands the right to be brilliant, celebrated and powerful. It's as if Germaine de Staël is challenging her readers to envisage a new order, a world in which traditional femininity and outsize genius walk hand-in-hand.

Here is Corinne's magnificent and rousing moral conclusion:

What else is happiness but the development of our abilities? . . . Is not killing yourself morally the same as killing yourself physically? And if mind and soul must be smothered, what is the point of going

on with a wretched life that stirs me up to no purpose? . . . Do not
people capable of great thoughts and generous feelings owe it to the
world to share them? Is not every woman, as much as every man,
obliged to make her way according to her own character and talents?
And must we forever imitate the instinct of the bees, one swarm
following another, without progress and without change?

In modern politics – in modern life – people routinely
divide themselves into separate, discrete compartments.
But Germaine de Staël – politician and artist – crashed
through the barriers between public and private life. She
explored the boundaries of femininity even as she reached
the heights of political influence. In doing so, it seems to
me that she expanded the range of possibility for all
women.

⚜

Germaine de Staël still poses a challenge.
I wonder if it matters, for example, that two hundred
years later a woman like me has more or less decided to
drop out? I don't mean that I was ever going to be a party
political player; that was never likely. Rather, that I might
have had opportunities to succeed within some influential organizations: certainly this was the case in the
Foreign Affairs and Trade Department. Large private busi-
nesses are also sites of modern power. Yet I have vacated
the field.
Believe me, as I roam around Paris, jobless, I'm conscious of the irony. I admire a woman who courageously
participated in public life, even as I retreat from it.
I can put my finger on one reason for my abdication. To
succeed in the major institutions of modern life, you need
to tolerate hierarchies. Our modern institutions were created

by men, and the model they used for them was the most
effective pre-modern organization – the military. It should
not surprise us that the greatest innovator of modern orga-
nizational structures was Napoleon himself. The civil service,
the European education and legal systems, chambers of
commerce – all made by Napoleon, all structured along
military lines, all based on hierarchy, bureaucracy and
accountability. These are admirable things in their way. I just
don't think they're me. Actually, I can't see Germaine de
Staël in a management consultant meeting either.

I recall a rather startling conversation with a male
friend. We were talking about women in large organizations, and why they don't do as well as they should. The
conversation rambled on, in the usual desultory fashion.
But suddenly it changed.

'Well of course,' my friend injected, out of the blue,
'there's also the fact that women are bloody nightmares.'

This rocked me. 'What on earth do you mean?'

'Well, men are tribal. They endorse the hierarchy. It's
like a footy team, or Shakespeare. You have the captain or
the king. He's the boss, right? What he says, goes. No one
challenges the leader's authority. But women, they just
won't accept authority.'

'Hmm,' I said dubiously. 'But what if you disagree with
the leader?'

'Well,' he said, 'you openly disagree, you openly humil-
iate the leader, only if you are prepared to challenge him
for the top job. You get the numbers, you mount a coup.
If you succeed, then you become boss and you get to
decide what happens. And if you're no good, someone in
turn topples you. It's a sensible process. Women,' he went
on sadly, 'they think it is right to disagree just because the
boss has done something stupid.'

Ah. Immediately about four incidents in my own career
sprang to mind. Times when I had gone to my male boss
and spoken up for what seemed to me basic good sense.
My views were tolerated and sometimes welcomed, but
I had always felt the ripple of masculine discomfort. Now I
understood what this meant. I was upsetting the order.
I was undermining the hierarchy. As Germaine de Staël
observed, *Women annoyed Napoleon as rebels . . .*

'You sheilas,' my friend continued, 'you're just not tribal.
You're anarchic!'

This man's ideas struck a chord with me. They certainly explained some of the perplexing interactions in
my own working life. And in a funny way they clarified
the strange impotence of the women politicians, the
ones who used to bustle in to see the Deputy Prime
Minister. Perhaps they seemed de-sexed because they
were de-sexed. They were playing a man's game, trapped
inside the hierarchy.

As I was musing on the implications of all this, my
friend suddenly changed tack once again. He was clearly
on a favorite topic.

'You know, of course, it's all about to change.'

'Huh?'

'The Internet is changing everything; it's creating a
more free and open world. The big organizations used to
control things, but not much longer. Now it's a networked
era. People can be independent; they can come together
if they have common goals. They don't have to put up
with the old tribal hierarchy, the old bureaucratic models.
This will suit women much better.

'God forbid,' he concluded ruefully, 'you'll probably all
take over.'

I didn't quite know what to make of this conversation

at the time, but now it's beginning to make sense. Germaine de Staël tried to navigate the perilous straits between the eighteenth and nineteenth centuries. Perhaps today we are in another period of transition, navigating our own straits of change.

As I sit here, an idea is coming to me, an image. It feels as if it has been floating around in the back of my head for some time, but is just coming into focus. My apartment has a small second bedroom. It's the place where I write and think, where all my books are shoved in messy piles on old bookcases. I have vaguely been thinking about working from this room, writing things for hire. And I've been faintly ignoring this idea because it seemed so, well, banal and inconsequential.

But perhaps it won't be so bad. I will be networked into the world and able to participate in it. Better still, I won't have to play some prescribed role any more: I will be answerable to no one. Maybe this will be my chance to integrate my private and public selves; to pull all the disparate parts together into one complete whole. And if I want to create a new self altogether, well, I can do that too.

Suddenly a notion arises that makes me smile, at my own ridiculous stream of consciousness as much as anything else. For the first time ever, my bedroom won't be a long, long way from the office: it will *be* the office. Where, perhaps, I'll have more power than I've ever had before.

I realize that I am sitting in the all-male café with a broad and goofy grin across my face, and the fat copy of *Corinne or Italy* facedown on my lap. The cigarette vendor behind the counter looks faintly surprised.

⚜

It's 1816. Napoleon, defeated and disgraced, suffers in lonely exile on the remote island of St Helena. His faithful Josephine is dead, passing away sweetly in 1814. The woman he married in her place, Marie Louise of Austria, has abandoned him and taken their son to Vienna.

On an impulse the former dictator picks up Germaine de Staël's novel *Corinne or Italy*. A novel he had tried to suppress. Perhaps he thinks the voice will have died down. Perhaps he thinks it will no longer hold its old infuriating power.

He turns the pages and the voice rings true and pure. The message is unmistakeable – a call to society, to women, to each woman, demanding that each and every one fulfil her gifts, that she *make her way according to her character and her talents*.

And it still drives him crazy. *I can see her, I can hear her, I can sense her, I want to run away, I throw down the book,* Napoleon rants. But he turns another page. And another. And still the voice continues, compelling, shimmering, vibrant. A siren song to liberty and love and art. He finds he can't stop reading.

However, I shall persist, Napoleon says, perhaps not realizing that he is admitting his own defeat. *I want to see how it ends, for I still think that it is an interesting work.*

⟢ 14 ⟣

A Good Death

I've always felt the great importance of getting into the right set at once on arrival in Heaven. The thing is, one must be careful in a new place not to get into uncongenial company.

Nancy Mitford

I'VE BEEN THINKING a lot about death. Oh, not in a negative way, quite the contrary. I've been thinking about death as the final act of the human narration, the ending that explains the beginning and the middle, the resolution that sorts it all out. It's a natural outcome, I guess, of thinking about women's lives, their whole lives, from beginning to end. In life, as in all good detective stories, it seems to me that a good ending can make sense of a messy plot, weaving all those loose threads and strange knots into a very satisfying whole.

Death is an honorable business in Paris. There are at least three cemeteries within the *périphérique*. Père

Lachaise is a major tourism destination, where little girls still put flowers on Marcel Proust's grave and young men make the pilgrimage to Jim Morrison's tomb. Parisians go there too. They like a good death – it suits the logical and pessimistic side of their nature.

And I too take a great interest in the topic. I realize that it's impossible to *plan* the way you die. But I do have some clear preferences. I would very much prefer *not* to die by animal. This applies particularly to shark or crocodile attack, which seems to me a most humiliating way to go. Humanity has spent an awfully long time overcoming nature, and I feel I would be letting the team down were I to slide down the evolutionary pole to the bottom of the food chain, being munched alongside plankton and seaweed. Rachel reckons she doesn't mind how she dies as long as it's not of lung cancer. Her reasoning is that if she tells her family and friends she has lung cancer they will secretly think it serves her right (or, more specifically, *serves her right stupid bitch!*) for smoking. This would be more than she could bear. On her death bed Rachel wants people to be nice to her – and mean it.

Some people prefer a quick death. My present preference is for a slow one, with time for tender goodbyes and little speeches and farewell parties, and, well, last words, and final says on the matter. Whatever the matter might be.

So here I am standing at Place de la Concorde. As usual I have the best intentions of strolling around and looking at the gorgeous, gilded sculptures and flowing fountains. As usual I find myself paralyzed at the thought of moving anywhere off this bit of footpath for fear of the traffic that swirls in a chaotic frenzy. So I shall just swivel and gaze and think.

Even with the traffic, this is still one of the most beautiful and famous locations in Paris. Place de la Concorde means harmony and amity and peace. Ceremonial festivities are still held here. But this is also the killing field of Paris; this place is stained with blood.

During the Revolutionary Terror, from 1793 to July 1794, no less than 1,119 people were executed here. But you wouldn't know it. There are plaques everywhere in Paris commemorating all kinds of people and events. But there is no plaque here to remind us of the shaved heads and tied hands, the ugly open tumbrel, the jeering crowds, the smell of stale blood, the sweat and fear on the platform. Perhaps it was just too horrible.

In those dark days, it was fashionable to laugh at the guillotine. People were careful with their final words. On approaching her death, Manon Roland, one of the republican salonnières, cried out magnificently: *'Sweet Liberty, what crimes are committed in thy name!'* In a different style, the revolutionary Danton quipped roguishly to the executioner: *'Show my head to the people! – it is worth the trouble.'*

But not everyone was like that.

On 15 October 1793, Queen Marie Antoinette was brought here to die. She had spent her final days in solitary confinement in the Conciergerie prison on the Ile de la Cité. If you have been to the Conciergerie you'll know just how surprisingly awful it is. It makes you shiver. It makes the hair stand up on your neck. And it's not just the cold. Even after two hundred years, the pale stones reek of horror.

Just after 11 am the executioner arrived at the Queen's little cell. He tied her hands behind her back and hacked off her hair. She climbed awkwardly into the open tumbrel. The wooden benches were hard beneath her thin white gown. The cart rumbled over rough cobblestones down the length of rue Saint-Honoré. At rue Royale it turned left to reach the open Place. The revolutionary artist Jacques-Louis David was living in rue Saint-Honoré and saw the Queen pass by. He quickly sketched what he saw: an ugly, shrunken and devastated woman.

After she died, the Queen's surviving friends were haunted by thoughts of the long, lonely hour she endured in the cart. What was she thinking as she confronted the taunts and stares of her former subjects? As she was carted like cattle to her death?

Along the route the Queen glimpsed reminders of other days. She passed the rue Royale apartment she had kept for her private visits to Paris. Maybe she remembered the fun of those jaunts to masked balls and the opera, the company of friends, the thrill of escaping court duties.

As she turned into this Place, she may have recalled her very first public event in Paris after she married the heir to the throne and became *Dauphine*. It took place in May 1770 when this was known as Place Louis XV. Nearly 300,000 had turned out to greet the newlyweds, but the event was badly managed and 132 people died in the crush. Marie Antoinette's second visit to Paris was more successful. The crowd cheered the young couple and the Duc de Brissac told the young *Dauphine* that all of Paris had fallen in love with her. Marie Antoinette wrote about the event to her mother, Empress Maria Theresa of Austria, remarking complacently how little seemed required of her in order to please the crowd. Her mother wrote back and sharply told her daughter not to take anything for granted. Mother, it turned out, knew best.

But perhaps Marie Antoinette had other, more somber recollections in mind. After all, she had changed a lot over the past few years. From a spoiled, haughty creature she had transformed into a strong and loyal woman. She stood by her husband, refusing to leave the country without him. She had comforted him and cared for their children with a steadfastness that few who knew her thought possible. But her husband, the King, was now dead, guillotined in January. She had been humiliated during a show trial when she had been accused of all kinds of crimes, including incest with her own son. The little boy had been removed from her care. She had heard him swear and curse as the guards had taught him, and sing revolutionary songs in the courtyard.

Whatever her private thoughts, Marie Antoinette retained her aristocratic *hauteur* to the end. She held her head high. As she crossed to the guillotine she inadvertently stepped on her executioner's foot. '*Pardon, Monsieur,*' she said, with Hapsburg precision, '*I did not do it on purpose.*' It may have been a statement about her whole foolish, tragic life.

Of course, the death of a queen lends itself to drama. And I have a literary turn of mind. I am all too inclined to elevate small incidents into grand gestures, to read Shakespearean significance into events which are no more than the sheer bump and accident of life.

Which brings me to a very different death. Two months after the execution of Queen Marie Antoinette, Louis XV's mistress, Jeanne du Barry, followed the same route from the Conciergerie to this Place. She too had begun her career here. She was a pretty twenty-year-old mingling in the crowd on the day they unveiled Louis XV's statue in 1763. It was, by coincidence, the day that Madame de Pompadour made her last public appearance. The beautiful blonde successor to Madame de Pompadour was spotted by Jean du Barry, cardsharp, impresario, dealer and pimp. He would marry Jeanne, introduce her to the top men in Paris, and eventually take her to Versailles to captivate Louis XV himself.

But, on the way to her death, the sunny, racy past must have seemed an eternity away to Madame du Barry. It was a freezing December afternoon. Snow was falling and the light was dim. Most of the crowd had given up and gone home. But the bloodthirsty and the curious stayed to gawk at the famous beauty who had captivated the former King. What they saw was a plump, frightened fifty-one-year-old woman. Even this hardy crew was shocked and disturbed by her frantic moans and sobs. An anxious murmur started up.

Right up until the very last moment, Madame du Barry couldn't believe this could happen to her. She had loved life, and life had been rich and full of glories undreamt of for a little Parisian girl. She couldn't believe it would end like this, why should it? Was she not simply one of the people? Until the last moment, she begged and bribed and pleaded. *'I'll show you where my jewels are, there's more to tell, wait,'* she said. The night before her execution she ate an enormous meal, as if she couldn't get her fill of life's sustenance. The next day when they came to get her she was amazed. *'This can't be happening, it's a mistake, wait, please.'* As they placed her in the tumbrel she stumbled and wept. She was a woman who loved life and wanted to keep on living, no matter how briefly. As they rumbled over the cobblestones she moaned and begged. As they pulled her onto the platform she struggled and pleaded and wriggled. As they lay her down, positioning her head in the crevice of the guillotine, she said – and these were her last words: *'Wait, Monsieur, I beg you . . . just a minute more!'*

I don't take a moral view about how a life should be lived or ended. If anything, I take an aesthetic view. I realize it's impossible to control the circumstances of death. But a good death surely lends poetry to a life. Marie Antoinette's death was moving because she was a woman who transcended herself at the end. Madame du Barry's death was touching because she didn't.

⚜

I turn and stroll back down the rue de Rivoli. At the Galignani bookshop I stop and idly turn to a table of French-language paperbacks on sale. A title catches my eye: *Amoureuses du Grand Siècle* (Gallant Women of the Great [17th] Century). Mmm, interesting. I turn to the table of contents. Here is Ninon de Lanclos. Here is Madame de Lafayette. And here is the woman whose ultimate fate has eluded me, Hortense Mancini, la duchesse Mazarin.

I flip to the relevant chapter, and then straight to the last page. It says: *He* [her husband] *deposited her coffin next to that of her uncle Mazarin in the funeral monument in the College of Four Nations founded by the Cardinal, today our Institut* [de France]. This is nothing new. I knew this. But I went to see, and the body's just not there.

I read on: *One would like to imagine the ghost of the joyous Hortense presiding over the debates of our Académiciens.* Yes, that's right, I think. One *would* have liked to imagine the ghost of Hortense at the Institut. But she wasn't there.

And then, with leaping heart: *But in 1793 her remains were thrown into the Seine by the sans-culottes* [revolutionaries].

I am transfixed, rooted to the spot, electrified by this
bulletin. So *that's* what happened to Hortense. I can hardly
breathe.

It happened in the exact same year that Marie
Antoinette and Madame du Barry died. At the height of
the Terror. Just over the river the rabble must have
somehow stormed the Institut and extracted the – the
what? coffin or bones? – from the tomb and thrown
them into the Seine. (I wonder why they didn't do the
same to the remains of Cardinal Mazarin?) And then the
bones must have just flowed down through the city like
so much debris. Perhaps the remains of Hortense
mingled with the blood of those who died on the guillotine. Strange to think that Hortense Mancini played a
part in French history – nearly one hundred years after
her death.

I look around, wishing there were someone here to tell.
All of a sudden I feel very emotional. I feel as if I too am
part of this flow, this river of life and death, this beauty and
this futility, these women.

If history were an emotion, perhaps this would be the
feeling.

⚜

Père Lachaise is not what I expected. I imagined it would
be quiet and peaceful. But it certainly doesn't feel dead. In
fact, it's alarmingly alive. Everywhere I look the head-
stones have cracked and the rubble is piled up and green
growing shoots poke through the dirt. It's as if a slow-
moving earthquake were underway. In fact, it's rather as if
the dead themselves were restless, shifting and squirming
under the earth, gradually easing their way to the surface.
A few staff members stand around with shovels. They have

a helpless expression, as if overwhelmed by the struggle to keep the buried in their rightful place.

And looking at the list of inhabitants here, I can see why. These were larger-than-life figures – larger than death too. Here's the taboo-breaking Colette lying under a short square slab, with fresh flowers on her grave. Here's Edith Piaf, the heartbreaking and heartbroken singer. Maria Callas, who died of sorrow when Ari Onassis married the widow Kennedy. The great actresses Simone Signoret and Sarah Bernhardt. Cléo de Mérode, the nineteenth-century *cocotte* who befriended the young Colette. *Gloria in excelsis Cléo!* her lovers would sing appreciatively. Marie Laurencin the painter: Coco Chanel once commissioned and then rejected a portrait by Laurencin; the artist portrayed Chanel as soft, sweet and dreamy – quite unlike the woman herself. Marie d'Agoult who ran off with Franz Liszt. Dancing Isadora Duncan who died of a scarf. All these women are buried here. Even so, they don't seem quite dead yet.

Père Lachaise is also the final home of some of the important men in these grand women's lives. As I approach Chopin's grave I see a small group of people kneeling and crossing themselves as they reverently place flowers and a Polish flag. They look so upset, you'd think Chopin died yesterday.

I seek out the grave of Germaine de Staël's lover Benjamin Constant. *In Arduis Constans* is carved on the tombstone. Constance in adversity. No doubt the motto is intended to signify a whole life, but I bet everyone who knew him thought it was an apt description of Constant's love affair with Germaine de Staël.

I am glad Benjamin Constant has a telling phrase on his tombstone. Most of the gravestones are very dull, offering merely a date of birth and death. I rather like the idea of something witty on my tombstone, something to make people laugh, or think. In my deepest secret fantasy I imagine it also says something like: *Here lies Lucinda Holdforth – diplomat, author, showgirl.* I have no idea how I am going to justify showgirl.

But if Père Lachaise is short on witty words, it does have some good visual jokes. Here's President Felix Faure, who died in 1898 while making love to his mistress. He's on his back, a life-sized statue reclining on his tomb. And he's got a very pleased look on his face – it's almost post-coital. Marshal Suchet was one of the bravest of Napoleon's marshals. Above his grave is a busty angel caressing an erect cannon.

A well-dressed man minces his way down a path. He leads me unerringly to the defiled tomb of Oscar Wilde; gentle, brilliant, persecuted Oscar Wilde. Oscar loved Paris. The city revealed to him the flipside of beauty, the price to be paid for pleasure, and the exquisite moment when pleasure flirts with danger. The Parisian aesthetes inspired *The Picture of Dorian Gray*, one of my favorite books. Paris in the late 1900s was completely unlike triumphal, brutal, imperial London. Having been defeated by the Germans in 1870, Paris was a city at home with frailty. It had a vocabulary for failure. Delicate and painful emotions like *tristesse, ennui,* regret and even disgust could be explored in this city without shame. No wonder it was where Oscar Wilde retreated to die.

Rachel has an interesting view of Parisian decadence. She thinks Paris hides her dark side, her twentieth-century failures, the stain of Nazi occupation and collaboration. Official, glorious, gilded Paris, she thinks, obscures the darker truths. In her blacker moments Rachel calls Paris *the museum theme park* or, even more cruelly, *the real Euro*

Disney. She says these things with a scornful turn of her curved lips.

There are lots of people who think it's unhealthy to dwell on death or dying or even the past. They reckon that the thing to do is to live for today and to look steadfastly into the future. And I've learned my own lesson about living in the past.

When my boyfriend left me after the 1996 election, I didn't believe it. I was absolutely convinced that he had suffered some kind of brainstorm from which he would, eventually, recover. And when he recovered, I thought, he would hurry back to me and we would get married and live happily ever after. This belief was so strong that it was only slightly shaken when he went off on his diplomatic posting to Jakarta. Four months later I was still calling and e-mailing him, waiting with anxious but unquenched faith for the inevitable moment of his return.

One day a mutual acquaintance came to see me. He brought up the subject of my boyfriend. 'Well of course it's so lonely for him up there,' I said. 'It can be awful you know.'

'That's not what I heard,' he replied, looking at me from under his eyelashes. Then he glanced down and added, 'Of course, they're still keeping it pretty quiet.'

I rushed around to visit two dear friends, a couple, on whose old blue couch I collapsed as great shiny tears spouted from my eyes. I couldn't believe it. This man was my destiny! Joanne hugged and consoled me. But her husband took a different approach. 'So let me get this straight,' said James, leaning forward, pushing his glasses back on his nose. 'You say that you and this guy were meant to be together. But you say he's not only left you. He's left the country. He's got another job. And now you are telling me he's even got another girlfriend.' James looked straight at me, with an incredulous look on his face as if he couldn't quite believe he was about to state something so obvious. 'I mean, face it: *it's over.*'

Once I stopped crying I felt a lot better. And I started to recover almost immediately.

But if personal history can be unhelpful, History with a capital H is entirely meaningful to me. I suspect it has replaced literature as a way for me to learn what it means to be human. Today we lead formless lives. We live with limitless freedom in a world without contours. History, and her sister, tradition, offer us the shape and style of human experience. It's the standard against which we can choose to measure ourselves, or rebel.

There's another reason. It's only when you understand history that you can appreciate how culturally determined we all are. Things which we tell ourselves are 'natural' are often nothing more than behavioral fads. For example, I am, historically speaking, a late Romantic, that's my historical fate. But it doesn't mean I have to confine my-self to the limits shaped by my age.

I once made the mistake of telling my boyfriend that I didn't want a small, meager life but dreamed of a big one. At that time I really didn't know what I meant myself. If I could have expressed it I would have said it wasn't about a grand style of living, or travelling widely, or even about doing adventurous things. In fact, it wasn't about external things at all. It was about a desire for an enlarged sense of life, an internal spaciousness, a capacity for fullness of experience and response.

My boyfriend simply scoffed at me, he thought I suffered from a bit too much self-esteem. He came from an upright Protestant family which prized financial security and modesty and solid achievement. He thought I was a grandiose Irish Catholic with jumped-up views and romantic delusions. Perhaps he was right.

⚜

Wandering and dreaming, losing myself in the alleys and corners of Père Lachaise, today I sense a deep connection to the women of Paris. I am grateful to the city that nurtured them and welcomes me.

This Paris, the Paris I love, feels handmade to me, delicately stitched together through time. It's like a lovely collaborative work of art, initiated by the seventeenth-century salon hostesses, enriched by their eighteenth-century successors and embellished in turn by their nineteenth- and twentieth-century descendants. Each generation of women adding to the legacy before handing it on. Like a beautiful tapestry woven by dozens of hands over hundreds of years.

I stand here suffused with memories not my own, and yet it seems that they belong to me as well.

At the end of my long walk around Père Lachaise, I come to the top of the hill. Here is Gertrude Stein's grave. It is massive, plain and strong, like the woman herself. GERTRUDE STEIN spell the big gold letters. After a moment I walk around the back. There, in much smaller letters, is the other name. Alice B. Toklas.

I'd heard about this grave, and, no doubt like most people, I thought how appalling it was that Alice was relegated to afterthought status. But in fact, the inscription was at her express request. Which suggests a kind of pride in modesty. It's as if Alice is saying to us: Behind every great woman, there's . . . another great woman.

~ 15 ~

Au Revoir

It seems that our mind, our temper, passions, taste and
feelings are influenced by the places where we dwell.

La Bruyère

RACHEL AND I are drinking champagne. I love champagne. I *really* love it. The 'thwop!' as the cork pops. The
burble of the pale liquid as it rises up the long delicate
flûte. The tingling 'chink' of the clinking glasses. The first
sweet heady rush as the liquid aerates the blood. I never
get bored with the little rituals. And I love the legends of
champagne, so many of which are associated with women.

The most famous of the champagne dames was Lily
Bollinger. She's the one who said of champagne: *I drink it
when I'm happy and when I'm sad. Sometimes I drink it when
I'm alone. When I have company I consider it obligatory. I trifle*

*with it when I'm not hungry and drink it when I am. Otherwise
I never touch it – unless I'm thirsty.*

I knew this quote for many years, and developed a
completely idiosyncratic mental image of its originator.
In my mind's eye Madame Bollinger was a French
version of Morticia Addams – slender and willowy,
possibly sporting a long cigarette holder. Then I saw a
photo of the real thing. Here was a stout working
woman with thick ankles and bushy hair, riding a bicycle
through her vineyards.

After a moment's mental readjustment, I liked the
reality even better than my imaginings – an old lady
cheerfully popping a bottle at afternoon tea-time. There
were other champagne women too – and it may or may
not be pertinent to note that they were all widows. It's
hard to believe they weren't merry. There was most
famously the *veuve* (widow) Cliquot as well as Mesdames
Pol Roger, Pommery, Perrier and Roederer.

Hortense Mancini's best friend in London, St Evremond, is credited with introducing the British to champagne: he did so in Hortense Mancini's salon. Madame de
Pompadour didn't drink much, but she made an excep-
tion for champagne. She thought, *Champagne is the only
wine that leaves a woman beautiful after drinking it.*

For the past few days we've been at play. Rachel has
barred me from old museums and historic buildings.
Instead we have preened in the Café Beaubourg and
posed at the China Club. Rachel bought chunky shoes at
Freelance and groovy knits at Joseph, and I bought a pair
of sunglasses at Karl Lagerfeld's gallery shop and a pair of
red skin-tight gloves from a century-old *gantier*. We
explored the glorious nooks and crannies of the Marais
district. We took a long afternoon tea at Mariages Frères.

But now this is my last night in Paris and Rachel and I are drinking in the bar of the Brasserie Alcazar. We're talking about the future. She's decided she's had enough – she's had a job offer and she's going to move to London. 'Look, there are a lot of things about this place that get to me,' she says, 'but the main thing is: I need to live in English!'

Actually, I know what she means. I've got language troubles of my own. For years now I have been writing in the voice of men and in the language of men. Speeches for men like the Deputy Prime Minister, papers for management consultants. To earn a living in my second bedroom I shall probably have to continue speaking in the voice of men. But somehow I want to find a way to express myself in my own voice. Discover what a modern woman's voice is like. Discover what *this* woman's voice is like.

⚜

It's the following morning and slightly hungover, dark glasses in place, Rachel and I set out for our last long sunlit walk through Paris. We walk down the rue Vieille du Temple, across Pont Louis-Philippe, across Pont Saint-Louis, behind Notre-Dame, and then over the Pont de l'Archevêché to the Left Bank. It's Rachel's favorite walk in Paris and I can see why. Every step is beautiful. As we cross the bridges the Seine flows beside and under and around us.

And so – it seems inevitably – we wind up at Shakespeare and Company bookshop where the wordy young Americans squat on benches, boxes and chairs; where the dust rises and falls on thousands of unsold books; and where once, on my first visit to Paris, an ex-lover from Australia recognized me by the sound of my voice.

I head straight over to the bookshelf full of old Paris guidebooks. One of them has a red hardback cover and gold print. It's called, simply, *Paris*. It is by André George and was published in 1952. I flick through it, admiring the plentiful black and white photos of the great buildings and cityscapes, the gloved women and snub-nosed Citroëns. Then I come to this: *Of great moment in the history of France is the Rue de la Victoire, named to commemorate Bonaparte's victorious campaign in Italy. He used to live at No. 60, in the hôtel of the young and unattached widow Josephine de Beauharnais . . .* Oops. I had taken Evangeline Bruce's word as gospel and looked for signs of Josephine's house at number 6. That's where I took Rachel on that dreadful rainy day when she was bored stiff. Now it appears that all along we were at *the wrong end of the street*. As Rachel approaches I snap the book shut. 'Anything interesting?' she asks. I shake my head casually. 'Not really,' I say. I quietly buy the book and stuff it discreetly into my bag.

Finally we head back down to the Seine. The clouds have come over and a greenish tinge has returned to the sky and the water. The trees shake and roll in the wind. I look along the great panorama of bridges and buildings and monuments.

There are, of course, things I don't like about Paris. I don't care for the Pompidou Center. I am not keen to visit the new Bastille Opera House, although Rachel says it's great. And I have always refused to go up the Eiffel Tower.

But today I look at the Tower with new affection. There is a legend – who knows if it is true? – that Gustav Eiffel invented the garter belt. I used to think the Tower was an ugly phallic symbol, out of place in this beauteous, feminine, shapely city. But now when I look at it I see something different. A long, long *belle époque* leg encased in a fishnet stocking.

I remember Ellen saying to me once that no matter how many times she came, no matter how long she stayed, the rose-colored glasses never came off; that special Paris feeling never went away. 'You know, in Australia I am nothing special, but in Paris, they find me beautiful,' she said.

⚜

Australia could have been French. It was a close-run thing. French explorers like Bougainville, La Pérouse, d'Entrecasteaux and Baudin conducted important early research into Australian geography and botany. The Frenchman La Pérouse and the newly arrived English Governor Phillip literally bumped into each other on the shores of Botany Bay in 1788. The first printed reference to the term 'Australia' was by the French scientist Labillardière in 1804. And Matthew Flinders's celebrated maps of Australia relied in part on earlier French maps confiscated by the British. It was a sheer accident that the English saw a purpose – if you can call it that – for this great southern land before the French did.

Most astounding of all, perhaps, the young Napoleon Bonaparte applied to join La Pérouse's ill-fated expedition and was knocked back. It's hard to believe the future conqueror of Europe could have resisted the chance to attempt settlement in Australia. It's also strange to imagine that he might have died alongside his shipmates in the South Pacific, changing the course of European history.

In the end of course, Australia became part of the British Empire. We'll never know what might have been.

As if zeroing in on my thoughts, the young taxi driver leans his head back and asks me where my flight is going. I tell him Australia.

'Ostralia,' he repeats excitedly, 'I adore zis country!'

I can't help but smile. 'Really? What do you adore about it?'

'*L'éspace!* It's so spacious and free, you know?'

'Yes I do. Have you been?'

'But of course! Right now I am saving up to go back zere. I woz on ze Golden Coast. I zed to myself: What if all ze people here were speaking French, zis would be Paradise!'

I tell him I come from Sydney.

'Sydney! Ah,' he shakes his head regretfully, ponytail swinging, 'Our explorers were not zo smart. We did not get Sydney. Instead we got *Nouvelle Calédonie.*'

Suddenly the thought of his nation's historic miscalculation sets him rocking with laughter.

⚜

Many people hate flying. It's not just the fear. It's the infantilization enforced by airline routines – the endless instructions, the baby food, the imposed sleep. But I don't mind. I rather enjoy being airborne, feeling timeless and weightless. These air stewards can boss me around all they like. I settle into my seat and tune into my interior world. In the noisy vacuum of the cabin it's easy to hear myself think.

People like to quote the famous Ernest Hemingway line that *Paris is a moveable feast*, as if the memory of Paris alone is enough to satisfy. If Paris is a feast, then I'm still hungry. I haven't yet had my fill: in fact, I doubt I will ever be sated. That's why I'll just have to keep coming back.

And I'm sure the city will always welcome me, no matter what my stage of life. I can't see myself returning to, say, Mexico or China as an old lady. But I can see myself in the teashops of Paris, still perfectly at home. Paris has, after all, been meticulously constructed by intelligent women for their pleasure. There's even a graceful language for a woman's evolution: she might arrive in Paris as a fresh-faced *ingénue*, grow through experience into a *femme du monde*, try out her style as a *femme fatale*, and wind up as a *grande dame*.

Before I came to Paris I had been only too conscious of my messy life, with its mistakes and false starts. The past lacked grace; the future lacked purpose.

But over these last three weeks I have had the privilege of inhabiting other lives. I've walked in the footsteps of the fabulous women of Paris. I've immersed myself in their city, stepping across the grand stage on which they played their greatest roles. Best of all, by gazing at the world through their eyes, I've seen a woman's life in a new way. My frame of reference has forever expanded. It's as if I was trapped in a small room and discovered the door was unlocked all the time. As I venture into the fresh air, there is suddenly space and light and room to move.

In the Luxembourg Gardens there's a central octagonal pond where the children sail their model boats in the sunshine. Arrayed around the pond are no less than fifty white statues of the queens of various French regions. Up on their high white pedestals the women appear cold and remote, their eyes turned away from the colorful scene below.

Now I too have a gallery of grand women. These are not, however, haughty elevated creatures; they have stepped off the historical podiums and into my heart. My own personal advisory council of divas, artists, aristocrats and heroines, they will forever be there for me, to teach and tease, to spur and encourage, to inspire and console.

And to remind me that women can do anything, including create an entire culture that is the delight of the world.

And my messy life? I went to Paris fascinated by the art of living. I've come away seized by the notion of a life as art. When a woman wishes to construct her life she requires an inventive will, a conscious application to the task. But life can never be totally controlled. Inventing a life also demands a letting go; a gracious succumbing to the flow of time and the turn of dramatic events. It means being open and ready when the new phase is set to begin.

There's a line of Nancy Mitford's that means a lot to me. It's in her biography of Voltaire, called *Voltaire in Love*. She is referring to another amazing French woman, this time the scientist and intellectual Emilie du Châtelet, who was Voltaire's lover and companion for many years. The thought could be a reference to Nancy Mitford herself – or to me. Nancy Mitford wrote: *She was waiting, unconsciously, for that revolution which often comes in the life of a woman no longer young and directs the future course of her existence.*

I never guessed that a revolution could be so quiet.

My heart lifts and fills. At this lovely, shimmering, indeterminate moment in my life, poised in mid-air, the past and the future extend limitlessly before me. And I'm ready to embrace it all.

Further Reading

Harold Acton, *Nancy Mitford: A Memoir*, Harper & Row, New York, 1975.

Joseph Barry, *Passions and Politics: A Biography of Versailles*, Doubleday, New York, 1972.

Shari Benstock, *No Gifts from Chance: A Biography of Edith Wharton*, Penguin, New York, 1994.

Shari Benstock, *Women of the Left Bank: Paris 1900–1940*, University of Texas Press, Austin, 1986.

Bryan Bevan, *The Duchess Hortense: Cardinal Mazarin's Wanton Niece*, The Rubicon Press, London, 1987.

Anita Brookner, *Romanticism and its Discontents*, Viking, London, 2000.

Evangeline Bruce, *Napoleon and Josephine: An Improbable Marriage*, Phoenix Giant, London, 1996.

Edmonde Charles-Roux, *Chanel*, translated by Nancy Amphoux, The Harvill Press, London, 1995.

Edgar H. Cohen, *Mademoiselle Libertine: A Portrait of Ninon de Lanclos*, Houghton Mifflin Company, Boston, 1970.

Letters from Colette, selected and translated by Robert Phelps, Virago, London, 1982.

Colette, *Chéri* and *The Last of Chéri*, Penguin, London, 1954.

Colette, *Gigi* and *The Cat*, Secker & Warburg, London, 1953.

Colette, *My Apprenticeships* and *Music-Hall Sidelights*, translated by Helen Beauclerk and Anne-Marie Callimachi, Secker & Warburg, London, 1957.

Benjamin Constant, *Adolphe*, translated by Leonard Tancock, Penguin, London, 1964.

Benedetta Craveri, *Madame du Deffand and her World*, translated by Teresa Waugh, David R. Godine, Boston, 1982.

Vincent Cronin, *The Companion Guide to Paris*, Harper & Row, New York, 1963.

Vincent Cronin, *Louis and Antoinette*, The Harvill Press, London, 1974.

Pierson Dixon, *Pauline: Napoleon's Favorite Sister*, Collins, London, 1964.

Janet Flanner, *Paris was Yesterday*, edited by Irving Drutman, Harcourt Brace Jovanovich, New York, 1988.

Pierre Galante, *Mademoiselle Chanel*, translated by Eileen Geist and Jessie Wood, Henry Regnery Company, Chicago, 1973.

André George, *Paris*, Nicholas Kaye, London, 1952.

Maurice Goudeket, *Close to Colette*, Farrar, Straus and Cudahy, New York, 1957.

Cyril Hughes Hartmann, *The Vagabond Duchess: The Life of Hortense Mancini, Duchesse Mazarin*, George Routledge & Sons, London, 1926.

Joan Haslip, *Madame du Barry, The Wages of Beauty*, George Weidenfeld and Nicolson, London, 1991.

Selina Hastings, *Nancy Mitford: A Biography*, William Abrahams, New York, 1986.

John Hearsey, *Marie Antoinette*, Heron Books, 1969.

J. Christopher Herold, *Mistress to an Age: A Life of Madame de Staël*, The Bobbs-Merrill Company, New York, 1958.

Ruth Jordan, *George Sand*, Constable, London, 1976.

Linda Kelly, *Juniper Hall, An English Refuge from the French Revolution*, Weidenfeld and Nicolson, London, 1991.

Linda Kelly, *The Young Romantics: Their Friendships, Feuds and Loves in the French Romantic Revolution*, Random House, New York, 1976.

Madame de Lafayette, *The Princess of Cleves*, translated by Nancy Mitford, New Directions, 1988.

Philip M. Laski, *The Trial and Execution of Madame du Barry*, Constable, London, 1969.

Maurice Levaillant, *The Passionate Exiles: A dual biography of Mme Récamier and Mme De Staël*, Farrar, Straus and Cudahy, New York, 1958.

R.W.B. Lewis, *Edith Wharton: A Biography*, Vintage, London, 1993.

Axel Madsen, *Chanel: A Woman of her Own*, Henry Holt and Company, 1991.

André Maurois, *Lélia: The Life of George Sand*, translated by Gerard Hopkins, Jonathan Cape, London, 1953.

Dorothy McDougall, *Madeleine de Scudéry: Her Romantic Life and Death*, Methuen & Co, London, 1938.

James R. Mellow, *Charmed Circle: Gertrude Stein & Company*, Phaidon Press, London, 1974.

Yvonne Mitchell, *Colette: A Taste for Life*, Harcourt Brace Jovanovich, New York, 1975.

Nancy Mitford, *Madame de Pompadour*, Hamish Hamilton, London, 1954.

Nancy Mitford, *The Sun King*, Penguin, London, 1994.

Nancy Mitford, *Voltaire in Love*, Hamish Hamilton, London, 1957.

Nancy Mitford, *The Water Beetle*, Harper & Row, 1962.

The Nancy Mitford Omnibus (The Pursuit of Love, Love in a Cold Climate, The Blessing, Don't Tell Alfred), Penguin, London, 1974.

The Letters of Nancy Mitford, edited by Charlotte Mosley, Sceptre, London, 1993.

Christopher Ogden, *Life of the Party, The Biography of Pamela Digby Churchill Hayward Harriman*, Warner Books, London,1996.

Mona Ozouf, *Women's Words: Essays on French Singularity*, translated by Jane Marie Todd, The University of Chicago Press, Chicago, 1997.

Belles Saisons: A Colette Scrapbook, assembled and with commentary by Robert Phelps, Secker & Warburg, London, 1978.

Helen B. Posgate, *Madame de Staël*, Twayne Publishers, 1968.

Alan Price, *The End of the Age of Innocence: Edith Wharton and the First World War*, St Martin's Press, New York, 1996.

Joanna Richardson, *The Bohemians: La vie de Bohème in Paris 1830–1914*, Macmillan and Co, London, 1969.

Joanna Richardson, *The Courtesans: The Demi-Monde in 19th Century France*, Weidenfeld and Nicolson, London, 1967.

Joanna Richardson, *La Vie Parisienne 1852–1870*, Hamish Hamilton, London, 1971.

George Sand, *Indiana*, translated by George Burnham Ives, Academy Chicago Publishers, Chicago, 1997.

Madame de Sévigné: Selected Letters, translated by Leonard Tancock, Penguin, London, 1982.

Cornelia Otis Skinner, *Elegant Wits and Grand Horizontals: Paris – La Belle Epoque*, Michael Joseph, London, 1963.

Sally Bedell Smith, *Reflected Glory: The Life of Pamela Churchill Harriman*, Touchstone, New York, 1997.

Germaine de Staël, *Corinne or Italy*, translated and edited by Avriel H. Goldberger, Rutgers University Press, New Brunswick and London, 1987.

Gertrude Stein, *Paris, France*, Liveright, New York, 1970.

An Extraordinary Woman: Selected Writings of Germaine de Staël, translated by Vivian Folkenflik, Columbia University Press, New York, 1987.

Penelope Hunter-Stiebel, *Louis XV and Madame de Pompadour; A Love Affair with Style*, New York, 1990.

Judith Thurman, *Secrets of the Flesh: A Life of Colette*, Bloomsbury, London, 1999.

Louise de Vilmorin, *Madame de*, translated by Duff Cooper, Helen Marx Books, Canada, 1998.

Janet Wallach, *Chanel: Her Style and Her Life*, Nan A. Talese, New York, 1998.

Edith Wharton, *A Backward Glance*, Century, London, 1987.

Edith Wharton, *French Ways and their Meaning*, Restoration at the Mount and Berkshire House Publishers, Massachusetts, 1997.

Edith Wharton, *A Motor Flight Through France*, Northern Illinois University Press, DeKalb, 1991.

Andrea Weiss, *Paris was a Woman; Portraits from the Left Bank*, Pandora, London, 1995.

Noel Williams, *Five Fair Sisters at the Court of Louis XIV*, GP Putnam's Sons, New York, 1906.

Renee Winegarten, *Mme de Staël*, Berg, New Hampshire, 1985.

Acknowledgements

I am deeply indebted to all the team at Varuna – The Writers' House for the benefit of its development forum for works-in-progress and subsequent mentorship: special thanks to my mentor Margaret Simons. In London, thank you to Rachel Thompson. In Geneva, thank you to Ellen Hansen. In Paris, grateful thanks to the officials of the Institut de France and the Bibliothèque Nationale de France (Cardinal Richelieu); Madame Axelle Marois of the Ritz Paris; Monsieur Omar Guerida, proprietor of Chez Omar; le Professor Dominique Verdy of La Société des Amis de Versailles; and to Titi and Felix Boukobza. In Sydney, thanks to Sally Hone, Natalie Hoy and Rebecca Weisser and also to Clare, Michael and Justin Holdforth. At Random House Australia, many thanks to Jeanne Ryckmans and Nadine Davidoff. Thank you, Syd Hickman.